The Secret Life of Dog Owners

Also by Bruce Fogle

Interrelations Between People and Pets
Pets and Their People
Games Pets Play
Paws Across London
Know Your Dog
Know Your Cat
The Complete Dog Care Manual
The Complete Dog Training Manual
The Dog's Mind
The Cat's Mind
101 Questions Your Dog Would Ask its Vet
101 Questions Your Cat Would Ask its Vet
First Aid for Dogs
First Aid for Cats
The Secret Life of Cat Owners
Encyclopedia of the Dog

The Secret Life of Dog Owners

Bruce Fogle DVM, MRCVS

Illustrated by Don Grant

PELHAM BOOKS

PELHAM BOOKS

Published by the Penguin Group
27 Wrights Lane, London w8 5tz
Viking Penguin Inc., 375 Hudson Street, New York, New York 10014, USA
Penguin Books Australia Ltd, Ringwood, Victoria, Australia
Penguin Books Canada Ltd, 10 Alcorn Avenue, Toronto, Ontario, Canada m4v 3b2
Penguin Books (NZ) Ltd, 182–190 Wairau Road, Auckland 10, New Zealand

Penguin Books Ltd, Registered Offices: Harmondsworth, Middlesex, England

First published in Great Britain 1997
1 3 5 7 9 10 8 6 4 2

Typeset in 11.25/13.5pt Monotype Baskerville
Typeset by RefineCatch Limited, Bungay, Suffolk
Printed in England by Clays Ltd, St Ives plc

A CIP catalogue record for this book is available from the British Library

isbn 0 7207 2062 1

The moral right of the author has been asserted

CONTENTS

INTRODUCTION

Dogs are magnificent observers – better than we are. They are marvellous at reading our body language, which is why your dog may know without your needing to explain that you are taking it to the veterinarian, or that you are depressed or elated or even feeling a bit frisky. We humans have a rich vocabulary of body language but in our preoccupation with words and their meanings we've allowed our own instinctive understanding of body language to wither.

Dogs read us better than we read them, but that does not mean they understand *why* we behave the way we do. It may be that it is a very rare dog that *wants* to understand human behaviour but I would like to assume otherwise and have done so when posing and responding to the questions in this book.

Of course, no dog is really interested in why some owners deny the possibility that their dog might bite or bark or create havoc or why it has never learned the basics of urban living, but it might be interesting to some *people* why we behave the way we do with our dogs. That is what this book is about. During the twenty-seven years I have practised veterinary medicine there has been an explosion of information explaining our relationship with the natural world around us. The answers to the questions raised in this book are based upon the theories and musings of scientists around the world who are interested in our links with nature. They are also based upon hard scientific studies published in peer-reviewed journals.

Some of the reasons why we live with dogs are obvious. Dogs have better hearing than we do and can be trained to bark and defend our territory. But in other ways our reasons for sharing our homes with dogs are more complicated and often surprising. It is no secret that I'm an out-of-the-closet dogaholic. I like them. I respect them. There are other facets, too, of our relationship with our 'best friend'; many of these are explored in the questions and answers that follow.

CHAPTER ONE

The Secret Instincts of Dog Owners

1. *Let's start with a simple one: who are better owners, men or women?*

It depends on what you want from life. If a dog wants to be one of the guys, to be part of a pack, to go out and do 'guy' things like headbutt other dogs, choose a man. If, on the other hand, it prefers a more gentle existence and wants to be mothered and worried over, a woman makes the best owner.

You might think these are sexist statements, but just look at the membership numbers of humane organizations. Animal welfare, animal rights, animal liberation – it doesn't matter which branch you examine, women make up about seventy-five per cent of members worldwide. This is not noticeable at first because, although women are the backbone of humane associations, token men usually run them. (When it comes to government, the media, big business or animal welfare concerns, men still get more respect. I once spoke at a university meeting in Sweden, where the role of women is as liberated as anywhere. After the meeting, a senior female faculty member stood and thanked me for journeying to Sweden, for saying what I said about the role of pets in society, but most of all for being a man. She had been making the same statements for years but it needed a man to say them for other men to listen.)

I am simplifying and stereotyping the sexes when I say that men are natural hunters and women nurturers, but it is not only our cultural values that impel women to become responsible for the care and welfare of family dogs. It is in their biology to do so. Even with working couples it is usually the woman who takes time off to take the dog to the vet. Her partner only shows up when serious decisions must be made.

Just like dogs, men like to form packs, to go drinking together, carouse together, go to war together. It is part of man's nature. Most dogs like to do active things like chase deer, kill rabbits, retrieve birds, fight with each other, eat meat – and so find great enjoyment living with men. But if a canine wants a quieter life, enjoys being groomed, likes knowing someone is always there worrying about it, a women is better. There is one minor risk with women however. Far more women than men are vegetarians and some of these women feel their dogs should be vegetarian too. This is a small sacrifice some dogs must pay for the benefits of living with the more considerate and caring sex.

2. *Why do both sexes feel safer when I'm around?*

This is a logical feeling. After all, dogs hear better than people and, through their own instinct, bark to let the rest of the family know that danger is lurking. That instinct has been exaggerated through selective breeding and careful training.

But there is instinct too in this human feeling of security and its genesis is in human evolution. For the survival of the fittest, avoiding danger is as important as eating and mating. Prehistoric people did not have any better hearing or vision or ability to smell than people do today but the smartest of them had the common sense to pay attention to the behaviour of animals that surrounded their living sites. These animals, with their superior senses, were aware of the approach of the pro-verbial sabre-toothed tiger before people were. Small animals warned people of the presence of danger from larger animals, or, for that matter, of the danger from groups of other people. Over millions of years, people's brains developed circuitry that told them that animals in flight, or the absence of ani-mals, are signs of danger. People were not alone in developing this 'instinct'. Other primates also use other animals to warn of predators. In the course of evolution, co-existing with ani-mals was a precursor to survival. Throughout their evolution, from the campsite to permanent settlements, to and through the development of agriculture, people lived in close proxim-ity to animals. Only now, when most people in the developed world live in a post-agricultural environment, have they been cut off from animal contact.

A vestige of this evolutionary development still exists which is one of the reasons why virtually every single culture throughout the world keeps animals of one type or another. In a sense, dogs take advantage of this part of human instinct. People instinctively feel safe in the presence of other animals with superior senses and have learned through experience that dogs are genuinely good to have at their feet. The dog fits instinctive and pragmatic safety requirements very nicely, which is why, in only 15,000 years – a mere fraction of a second in the history of evolution – it has become the world's favourite human companion.

3. *I walk on all four legs. I bark. I'm completely covered in fur. I've got fabulous canine teeth. They know I'm a dog so why do they still think of me in human terms?*

People can't help it. All their terms of reference are human. Hard as they try it is simply impossible for them to think in any terms other than human. Not that it's such a bad thing. Using human experience to describe dog behaviour is scientifically quite reasonable but occasionally anthropomorphism, as it is called, can go too far. In her sometimes riveting book, *The Hidden Life of Dogs*, Elizabeth Marshall Thomas stretches the point a little too far when she uses human cultural terms to describe dog behaviour: 'Mischa had married my daughter's husky'; 'From the moment Violet set eyes on Bingo, she adored him'; 'After they mated they turned to each other, began to kiss, then to frisk around the room. Bingo rejoiced with them in spirit'; 'She fell into a fitful sleep and dreamed of her own infancy'.

People find it almost impossible to avoid using human terms to describe dog behaviour, but make a mistake when they apply human ideas like marriage to dogs. Certainly, dogs dream. They have rapid eye movements (REMs) and electrical changes in their brains that are identical to those of humans when they dream, but people can only guess what dogs dream about. A degree of anthropomorphism is inescapable. It is a profound and positive component in the relationship people have with their pets and it is an undercurrent in owners' fantasies about their pets. Only antiquated 'cause-and-effect' scientists from an older, more rigid, scientific tradition feel uncomfortable with it. A level of anthropomorphism is perfectly acceptable, but there are limits. The

Czech writer, Karel Ciapek, was reasonable in his assumptions when he wrote: 'If dogs could talk, perhaps we would find it as hard to get along with them as we do with people.' (Ciapek lived with Dachshunds, which might explain his attitude . . .)

4. *When I see a brush or comb I bare my teeth. I growl. I demand my independence. Why do they groom me so obsessively?*

Grooming is a social thing but it also defines who's in charge. Watch monkeys and you will see why. Nit picking is not just a hygienic measure to rid the body of parasites; when monkeys groom each other they are cementing social bonds. Monkeys only groom members of their own troop or group. So do people. People who do not have strong social bonds would never touch each other. This activity is restricted only to blood relatives, very close friends and sexual partners.

When people groom dogs they are carrying out simple hygiene, but they are also strengthening the glue that binds them together.

5. *Is that why I'm treated like their child?*

Yes. The modern dog is, in a curious way, a human artefact. Those people who originally selectively bred wolves and created dogs, bred for practical purposes: trainability, speed, barking. Curiously, they also selectively bred for larger frontal sinuses on wolves' heads, an anatomical feature of no practical or utilitarian value. They did not know it but they were instinctively breeding wolves to look both more intelligent and more juvenile.

A powerful human instinct draws people to the shapes and behaviours of young animals. The ethologist Konrad Lorenz, in one of his most famous articles, explained that the differences in form between babies and adults triggers different responses in people. 'Baby' shapes – large eyes, bulging craniums (or, anatomically speaking, enlarged frontal sinuses) and small chins – trigger the release of an automatic surge of disarming tenderness.

From the very earliest intervention in their breeding, dogs have been selectively bred to look more 'juvenile' than their forebears. Science calls this process 'neoteny'. Not only that, people selectively bred dogs to behave in a juvenile way. Their dependent behaviour has been most exaggerated in the last several hundred years. Crying, smiling, following, scrambling, crying to be lifted, clinging, lifting the arms or clapping the hands in greeting and approaching – all these are human infant behavioural patterns that instinctively stimulate a nurturing response from adults. All dogs, juvenile or adult, have many of these behavioural patterns too. (The naturalist Gerald Durrell called 'smiling' the dog's trump card.)

Breeding turned the wolf into a life-long wolf cub. Although they are chronologically adults, dogs remain both mentally and physically forever infantile – a clever evolutionary move on their part to trigger instinctive caring and nurturing from people. People have their own children and they too trigger a nurturing response from adults, but they grow up. In a sense dogs are superabundant child substitutes, unchanging, constant – forever cute and sweet in a dependent baby way.

6. *And is that why people gaze at me in such an intimidating way?*

People are unaware that they find it easier to look into a strange dog's eyes than a strange person's, and are often equally unaware that their unblinking stare is a sign of intimidating dominance.

Infants stare, but by the time they reach school age both their instincts and their experience have taught them to avert their eyes. This is one of the most powerful but unapparent behaviours that people have.

In adulthood, frank staring is frowned upon. Gaze is regulated, even within families. Just as with dogs, only the most dominant people are permitted to stare. This instinctive behaviour has existed in virtually all cultures and was perpetuated in some countries in modern times where commoners were not allowed to look upon their king.

Instinct and learning regulate how long people may stare at other people, but staring is rewarding. That is why films and television are so popular; viewers can gaze as long as they want. That is also why the living environment is so appealing. By shifting their attention outward from themselves, by watching and listening, people lower their state of arousal. Nature encourages unlimited looking and dogs are part of nature. Dogs virtually invite people to gaze upon them and when people do they feel more relaxed. In human relations this is a personal freedom limited by instinctive and cultural constraints.

7. *I come from a long line of carnivores who killed to survive but in my own lifetime I've never killed anything larger than a moth. Why do they expect that I will instantly defend and protect them without any training?*

Although some dogs seem to have travelled a great distance from their wolf origins, people still think their own dog, regardless of its shape or size, will defend and protect just as a member of a wolf pack will come to the aid of another member when it is attacked. There is a grain of truth in this idea but there are more complicated and hidden reasons why people think their dogs will protect them.

Strange as it seems, although outwardly dogs are like human children, dependent on their owners for food, security and good health, in a curious way there is a reverse side to the relationship. Subconsciously, the relationship flips. It sounds impossible but dogs become the parents and people become the dependents.

When a child is born it depends so completely on its mother that for the first year or more of life it doesn't even consider itself to be independent from her. The human baby is 'merged' with the mother. Mother provides warmth, nourishment and protection. When the baby touches its mother, its sense of arousal diminishes. It becomes calm. Its heart rate slows, its skin temperature drops, its blood pressure returns to normal. Mother means contentment and security.

A little later in life the baby begins to realize that it is a unique being and begins to separate from its mother. Some people call this stage the 'terrible twos' because it often leads to frustration – tantrums and crying – as the baby enters the first stage of true independence. The feeling of security that mother provides remains, but it becomes altered by the realities of life. A typical grown son understands that at least physically speaking he is now more capable of protecting his mother than she is of protecting him.

That reality does not seem to enter the feeling of dog owners towards their dogs. It does not because, in a curious way, the dog provides some of the instinctive comforts that mother once did and these are based on touch.

If a person strokes a dog he or she does *not* know, the person's blood pressure and heart rate rise. But, if that person strokes his or her own dog, blood pressure, skin temperature and heart rate drop. The state of arousal diminishes. This only happens when a social relationship has developed between the stroker and the dog. Petting and stroking the soft, warm fur of a person's own dog stimulates the same physiological response that individual once had as a baby when he or she touched mother. In this context, psychologists call dogs 'transitional objects', providing warmth and security in the same way that teddy bears and security blankets do. Subconsciously, the dog offers the same feeling of security that mother did during the first eighteen months of life. Perfectly sensible people feel that their dogs will defend and protect them because, in the hidden subconscious life of the owner, the dog is the all-powerful and protective parent.

8. *Is that why they think I'm not as 'animal' as, let's say, foxes or wolves or coyotes. Why do they psychologically segregate me from my close relatives?*

People think of wild animals as 'species' but think of their dogs as 'individuals'. Wildlife shows on television portray animals following their instincts. Foxes steal eggs and bury them. Coyotes stealthily avoid human contact. Wolves lope through the woods, have disputes with each other, pounce on mice and eat berries, but are seen to follow their own wolf behaviour patterns. A television show might be about an individual animal but in a half- or one-hour television programme there is not enough time for the viewer to form a profound understanding of that individual animal the way a farmer, for example, understands each of his dairy cows.

People instinctively find the 'animal' in dogs appealing because this makes the dog part of nature. And just as people go for walks in the woods to 'feel better', so too living with a dog introduces nature into the human environment. A canine companion induces a state of relaxation, reduced anxiety and depression, heightened awareness and enhanced well-being. But dogs are not just part of nature.

I know a Yorkshire Terrier who, during the days following the introduction of a new pup into his home, gathered all his toys together – a rubber bone, a rag, a rawhide chew and a felt doll – and simply sat on them. This is a canine behaviour that his owners understood. To them he was doing a 'human' thing and in doing so the Yorkshire Terrier became a little less 'animal' and a little more human. People with dogs have the stimulating and exciting privilege of being front-row observers of how a completely distinct species thinks and behaves.

The fact that people happen to share a wide range of feelings, emotions and behaviours with dogs should not make dogs any less animal than their wild cousins. Rather, it should make people appreciate that a great range of animals share with them many feelings, emotions and attitudes that are thought to be uniquely human.

9. *Why does she trust me and confide in me more than she does in her own kind? After all, I can't even reply, other than just sit there and stare back.*

Exactly. It is because a dog does not answer back that it makes such a superb confidant.

Dogs are honest with their emotions, people are not. Dogs are truthful, people deceive. (Actually, it is not just people. Deceit is common behaviour among other primates too.) When people are young they believe what they are told. A promise is a promise. Later in life, whether it is in business or in love, people learn that what they hear is not necessarily true.

But at the same time they know that when it comes to their relationships with dogs, what you see is what you get. People learn that if a dog is unhappy with them it does not hide that fact. It sulks. If it wants affection it asks for it. If it is angry it does not suppress its anger. If it is joyous it does back flips. People trust dogs because dogs are blatantly honest. And that's why people confide in them, since the basis for truth is trust.

Sometimes people find the burdens of life overwhelming. Talking about what troubles them is the channel to their overcoming that torment or frustration. People value good listeners and some other people spend years in higher education to qualify as society's specially trained and licensed 'listeners'. These specialists often charge extremely high fees to act as non-judgemental listeners, to make eye contact, to concentrate, to be sympathetic, to listen. Dogs do this for a pat on the head and a crust of dry bread.

10. *What has a person's sex got to do with their relationship with me? Why is it that teenage girls are quite straightforward with me but teenage boys tease or downright abuse me?*

Some people like to think that these differences are created by the different expectations society has of boys and girls, but the answer lies deeper, in the hormonal and emotional differences between the sexes.

Hormonally, girls are born with sexually neutral brains. Boys are born with hormonally influenced masculine brains. In every mammal that has been studied, male babies produce male hormone just before they are born. This male hormone circulates in the baby's blood stream and affects the developing brain. Although the hormonal tap is turned off just before or at the time of birth, not to be turned back on again until puberty, this short jolt of circulating male hormone has served its purpose. It has primed the brain's development in a masculine direction. Girls are sugar and spice and all things nice because that's the way a neutral brain develops. Boys are frogs and snails, and in this context, puppy dogs' tails, because their behaviour has been influenced by sex hormone. Boys are naturally rougher in their play than girls and this applies to their behaviour with dogs. In psychological profiles, girls always show a greater interest in animals than boys and have more of a sense of responsibility towards them.

These differences are enhanced at puberty when serious hormone production begins. This coincides with a period in a young male teenager's life when he is most likely to abuse animals. Teenage boys in all cultures go through this phase, so much so that psychologists and psychiatrists think it is a

natural stage of male emotional and behavioural development. They argue that this is a vestige of the male's
evolutionary past. Men were the primary hunters while
women, burdened with the care of the young, were restricted
to gathering. To be a successful hunter, boys had not only to
understand animal behaviour but also to develop a ruthless-
ness, an ability to look straight into an animal's innocent eyes
then kill it. The teenage boy's inclination to kick dogs, and
particularly the inclination of gangs of teenage boys to kick
dogs, is but a remnant of evolutionary development. Dog
abuse by teenage boys also occurs because the abuser does not
yet have the maturity to understand the consequences of his
actions. He experiments in a simple, single-minded fashion,
oblivious to the dog's pain. This is different from dog torture
carried out by a pathological personality where torturing is
the actual reward.

Because girls evolved to perform other care-giving functions associated with nurturing, their relationship with dogs
does not involve this unpleasant period.

11. *I think my owners are gay. Does it matter?*

Yes. If a dog has gay owners it is, on average, likely to be better cared for than a dog that lives with a typical hetero-sexual couple. There are several reasons.

Homosexual male couples, unable to have natural children of their own, may make deep and profound emotional invest-ments in their dogs which, of course, can act as child substitutes. Caring for the dog bonds the couple in a common cause. They become classic 'parents' but in an exaggerated way, performing almost a caricature of heterosexual parenting. The relationship is deeply caring with the ever alert owners aware of the slightest change in the dog's behaviour. Gay male couples are careful about their dog's diet, hygiene and medical care. A dog that lives with a male homosexual couple is almost guaranteed superb consideration and attention although sometimes obsessively so.

Homosexual female couples also make better-than-average dog owners because they bring with them a double dose of caring and nurturing. In some circumstances a dog might find itself owned by gay females with strong masculine inclin-ations. The dog might discover that it is dressed in studs and leather and is named Vulcan or Mad Max but more often than not this is but window dressing, image projection. In the privacy of the couple's home, the dog reverts to the role of social bonder, glueing the couple together through their mutual interest in its wellbeing.

A final curiosity is the increased likelihood of parenting among dogs owned by gay couples. A remarkably high per-centage of dog breeders are homosexual couples, especially in the case of specific breeds such as toys or those with elegant coat textures and colours.

12. *I'm small. Whenever my owner picks me up and carries me close to her chest I hear her heart pumping. Why does she hold me so tightly and why is it almost always to her left?*

This is a common phenomenon and it is not related to left- or right-handedness in people. Almost eighty per cent of women instinctively hold their own babies to their chest with the baby's head close to their heart. Just as many people do the same thing with their dogs if the dog is small enough. While visiting the veterinarian and either talking or listening, many cradle their dogs in their arms, with the dog's head to the left and rock them as they would their own infants. Many male veterinarians become envious of dogs on these occasions.

13. *My owners have been married for several years and both work. They love me. Passionately. They call me their baby. So why don't they have a real human child?*

Life has changed. There was a time, in the very recent past, when men went off to work and women stayed at home to raise the children. Not so any longer. Women work because it is satisfying to do so or because two incomes are needed for the couple to live in the style they want. One consequence is that raising children is postponed but that does not eliminate the couple's desire to care for their own young. Enter the dog.

More than ever before, intelligent, educated, articulate couples acknowledge that their dog is their child substitute. These couples rotate who goes home at lunchtime to exercise the dog. When their jobs take them from one city to another – even from one country to another – it does not enter even the most distant reaches of their minds that they would re-home their dog.

The ready availability of dogs, the fact that a dog is such a rewarding family member, the chances to do things for it, play with it, care for it and attend to all its needs, only helps to postpone the time when these couples have their own children.

14. *Will life change for me after they have human kids?*

Probably. Most dog owners swear that life won't change for them or their dogs once children come along, then reality bites. There is no conceivable way that life does not radically change for people who have children. These changes apply to dogs too.

People quite correctly try to avoid any abrupt changes in their dog's routines but sooner or later changes must take place. There simply is not enough time to devote to a dog once a human baby is in the house. Babies can be quite exasperating and some people will take solace in the simplicity of the demands made by a dog. Dogs can become even more loved. More often, dogs become mild burdens, even threats. Wrongly, they suddenly may be denied access to the baby's room. If this is to happen, it should be done long before a baby comes home rather than as a direct result of the baby's presence.

One of the best times for any dog is when a baby is learning to feed itself. The most sensible dogs keep a low profile and learn to hang out around the high chair. This is a gratifying time of life.

As children grow, a dog finds new partners to play with but if a dog looks upon children simply as small people and therefore easy to dominate, then its life changes dramatically for the worse. Snapping at children is a just cause for punishment and dogs learn that it leads to reprimands, training sessions and sometimes abandonment. Even death penalties can be issued for dogs who dare to attack children.

More often, following the initially negative life changes of no longer being the centre of attention, as children grow up a dog finds that for the first time in its life it belongs to a true pack – parents, children and dog. It may find that life is more exhilarating but, curiously, this depends upon the social class of its owners. If a dog lives with a middle-class family it can expect to be played with more, comforted more and be a source of comfort more often than if it lives with a less well-advantaged family. It seems that in families lower down the social scale children don't know how to take advantage of a dog in their lives. This is more common with boys than girls. Girls, certainly those between nine and thirteen years old, according to one Canadian study, turn to their dogs for emotional support, contact comfort, protection and reassurance much more readily than boys.

Dogs become attachment figures for children and contribute to a child's basic sense of trust. But no matter how good dogs are in this role they can never replace parents or other people as resources for caring and learning. In the distressing circumstances of sexual abuse, children find dogs very supportive while they navigate their way through their feelings of isolation and confusion. Autistic children also treat dogs as extra special and display behaviour to them they don't display even to their families.

Many people feel that it is good for their children to be strongly attached to their dogs, but this is not necessarily so. According to Dutch psychologists, eight-year-old children who are strongly attached to their dogs have higher than average feelings of self esteem and self worth. Thirteen-year-old children who are strongly attached to their dogs have lower than average self esteem and self worth. Life changes for dogs after human children arrive but it changes for children too. A child's relationship with a dog can be a pointer to the development of the child's personality.

15. *And once their children leave home, what happens to me?*

That depends overwhelmingly on the personality profile of the new 'empty nesters'. Some parents yearn so much for the freedom and independence they experienced before having children that they long for the dog to depart from this life, leaving them free to come and go as they please and to travel at will.

Many people go through this phase but women in particular find the absence of being needed very stressful. Rather than relaxing into parental 'retirement', life becomes meaningless. This happens to men too, but to a lesser degree. For example, on a stress scale of mid-life changes, women rank the loss of contact with their grown children far higher than men do.

After the initial sense of loss, some people turn to their dogs for solace and comfort. The nest is empty but people have a lifelong need to nurture. Historically, parents continued to care for their young because their married children lived nearby. Grandparents were (and in many parts of the world still are) an integral part of the three-generation family. Historically they looked after the children while the parents hunted and gathered. With the dramatic changes in human lifestyles this century and the disintegration of the traditional family, the oldest generation no longer has the nurturing responsibilities it once had. In that sense dogs are lucky because they are the beneficiaries of this change. After children leave home, a dog can become the centre of attention which is, of course, exactly what a dog wants to be.

16. *I'm not complaining, I'm just curious. Why am I allowed to sleep in my owners' bedroom but their very own human children are not?*

Part of the answer is sex. Affluent middle-class couples enjoy having the privacy of their own bedrooms in which to do what they want. They don't want little Michael or Catherine popping up to ask what's happening. Dogs on the other hand, ask no questions. Usually, they sleep through any nocturnal human gymnastics although some dogs, especially young, active ones, get a vicarious thrill from standing on men's backs barking instructions. Amazingly, lots of people are willing to put up with this type of canine shenanigan. Some dogs, males in particular, get annoyed when people have sex. They feel very protective towards their female owner and become aggressive with men. These dogs are usually booted out of the bedroom for short periods of time but then allowed to return.

The reason why even nuisance dogs are allowed in bedrooms has ancient origins, when it was a case of survival of the fittest and people came to rely upon the hearing, scenting and night vision of other animals in order to survive. People still do this today with dogs. They allow, even encourage, dogs to sleep in their bedrooms because they feel safe. Even the tiniest Chihuahua is, in people's minds, a watch dog, a protector, a defender of the campsite. This is deeply ingrained human behaviour and it exists throughout the world wherever there are dogs.

CHAPTER TWO

The Secret Feelings and Emotions of Dog Owners

17. *Every single time she comes home she kisses me smack on the lips. I really enjoy her return – in fact I jump for joy. But why has she got this strange and, to be frank, unproductive habit?*

A dog serves a variety of roles but for many people, and for women in particular, dogs are there to be cared for, to be loved and nurtured. Even tough guys like Rottweilers and German Shepherds often get wet smacks on their foreheads and faces. Dogs of a similar size to human babies, like Yorkshire Terriers and Toy Poodles, get more kisses on the lips.

Women do this more than men but that doesn't mean men don't *want* to behave this way. It's just that in our culture some men are embarrassed to show their emotions. And yet, curiously, in public men are often more willing to show affection to dogs than they are to other humans. Strange as it seems, men often go to great extremes to avoid physical contact with others of their own kind in public. But they are just as willing as women are to pat, stroke and even cuddle dogs. 'New Men' even kiss their dogs in public.

People behave this way because, unlike virtually all other forms of life, they have a life-long need to care for living things. This has evolved out of the need to care for their own infants for a protracted period of time. Puppies, for example, have fully developed brains by the time they are twelve weeks old. By twenty-four weeks they can take care of themselves and soon they become competition for their parents. Human brains take infinitely longer to develop – some parts of the human brain need eighteen years to mature. In the survival of the fittest, nurturing was beneficial for both the parents and the young.

One of the problems people have, if you want to call it a problem, is that their need to nurture becomes universal. They care for their own families but they also care for other people, other animals, even plants. Kissing is just a visible sign of human caring. It is a relic behaviour because it no longer serves a practical purpose and this no doubt frustrates dogs. A mother's lips on a pup's lips is a sure sign of nurturing because the pup knows its mother is going to regurgitate something delightful for it. Humans may have done this in their evolutionary past and, in some cultures, mothers still do chew up food and pass it to their babies with a 'kiss'. But in the dog-owning Western world a human kiss will always remain symbolic rather than productive.

18. *I am a descendant of noble wolves and people know it. Why am I forced to wear a stupid ribbon in my hair?*

A ribbon is a minor inconvenience. Some dogs are forced to wear raincoats, hats, scarves, even boots and sunglasses. I've seen Pugs dressed as Sumo wrestlers, Chihuahuas in peach satin baby dolls, Whippets in Levi's.

Wolves have sufficiently dense coats of hair to protect them from being injured by vegetation and from the vagaries of inclement weather. Selective breeding diminished this protection for many dogs. Short-coated breeds like Dobermans, Boxers and Whippets really do benefit from added protection in very cold weather. Other breeds like Yorkshire Terriers, with excessively long facial hair, benefit from having the hair held out of their eyes with a ribbon. These are perfectly practical and reasonable reasons why certain dogs should be 'dressed' occasionally.

In many instances, however, dressing up is for the owner's satisfaction and has nothing whatsoever to do with the dog's physical wellbeing. It's simply 'playing dolls' and is a habit that is most indulged in in the United States and Japan, but especially in Italy. The British claim that dressing dogs is demeaning and will only do so for practical reasons. British weather, however, justifies the manufacture and successful sales of a wide range of 'country' clothing – for example waxed dark green jackets for dogs, identical to those worn by their owners who, through their clothing, proclaim they are 'country' people. In reality, the British are just as likely to dress their dogs as are others. Weather just gives them a plausible excuse.

By clothing a dog, subconsciously people are removing the

'animal' from their companion. It is one way of trying to make a dog more human. Just as with human babies, sex identification is colour coded – pink ribbons for bitches, blue ribbons for dogs. People who dress up their dogs, even when the clothes are seemingly justified by the climate, are, through their actions, emphasizing the emotional investment they are making in their canines. Unloved dogs remain undressed.

19. *My home is warm and food is always available. But what I really want to do is spend my day sniffing lampposts and rolling in horse manure. Why am I jailed? Why am I not let free?*

This is a relatively new phenomenon among dog owners and has its origins in the increasing feelings of responsibility conscientious people have towards both their dog's physical wellbeing and the feelings of other people in the community they live in. It's strictly a middle-class phenomenon.

There was a time, only a generation or so ago, when a dog was allowed to lead a dog's life. In the countryside, suburbia and small towns, many dogs lived in kennels in the garden or, if allowed in the house, were restricted to the kitchen. Each morning the gate was opened and the dog wandered off to do its own thing which, in most instances, was to smell lampposts and roll in horse manure. After all, this is the epitome of what most dogs want to do.

Unneutered males would get together in a benign 'brotherhood' and hang out at the home of the resident bitch in season. This 'pack' never acted as a genuine pack, hunting and eating together; each gang member returned home every evening for food and warmth, joining up again the following day to do a little scavenging, to sniff more lampposts and to look for bitches. Life was simple. Dogs had few behaviour problems because they were allowed to act like dogs.

But society changed. A major development was the replacement of horse power by car power. Naturally, this increased a dog's risk of injury in road traffic accidents but, more importantly, it dramatically reduced the amount of horse manure on the streets. Suddenly, dog droppings, a previously mild and inconsequential environmental inconvenience, became a social nuisance. In the absence of other excrement, dog droppings featured prominently on the landscape.

At the same time, dogs were invited to live in people's homes. Initially, to leave the kitchen and occupy all the floor space but then, almost surreptitiously, to climb on sofas and even beds. Today, in North America and Western Europe, about half of all pet dogs are allowed on their owners' beds. The smaller the dog the more likely it is to sleep with people.

This increasing intimacy has brought with it a greater feeling of attachment and responsibility on the part of owners. Conscientious owners feel a responsibility to their neighbours and try to control their dog's outdoor activities. More important is their emotional need to protect their dogs. That is why dogs are jailed. People think that by feeding them the best food and by providing creature comforts – warmth, soft mattresses and chewy toys – their dogs have landed feet first in heaven. They forget that these are but physical comforts.

Dogs have never been free. The actual concept of *dog* denies it. The dog is a human creation, bred under the control of people for their own purposes. What has happened in the latter part of this century is that, as people have developed stronger emotional attachments to their dogs, former limited canine freedoms have been eliminated and replaced by what people consider to be physical luxuries. As emotional dependency on dogs increases, their limited freedoms will be eroded further.

20. *When I was first introduced to my home, the adults told the children they had got me for them. Is it really true that I'm simply an amusement for the kids?*

Yes and no. Dogs are in part toys, different from dolls and teddy bears in that they bleed and die. Children graduate from having satin-edged blankets, to stuffed toys, to dogs. The unfortunate aspect of this development is that, although all of these items are deeply important to children, parents some-times think of each one as equally expendable.

Parents do get dogs for their children's amusement. After all, if the child is playing with the dog, the parent has more time to get on with other chores. However, it is very likely that although they do not precisely acknowledge the fact, parents are saying something important to their children when they bring a dog into the home. In this sense dogs are not simply childhood amusements.

Sensible parents tell their children that they are responsible for their dog. Unless a child is emotionally very mature, this is simply not true. Parents are responsible for the physical and emotional wellbeing of family dogs. Yet this standard parental proclamation is often the first intimation children have of their responsibility for other living things. When a parent introduces a dog into the home saying, 'It's for the children', what he or she is really saying is 'I think parenting is important and I want my child to start parenting now'. In all cultures, from wealthy and sophisticated to more primitive and basic, women and children are responsible for pets. In hunter/gatherer societies, children learn about animal behaviour at least in part through pets. In our society they have an early opportunity to learn about their later responsibilities to the living world around them.

21. *But I'm a dog. I have feelings and emotions. I pine if I'm left alone. Why should I be treated like a stuffed toy or a learning experience?*

Because, until very recently, most people denied that dogs were aware of their own feelings and emotions. Many still find it difficult to accept that dogs have emotions. They like to think that every response a dog makes is instinctive, a reflex wired by evolution into its brain. They like to think that dogs work on autopilot, without too much thinking or feeling. Veterinarians know that dogs have feelings and emotions, in part because they have had the opportunity to observe so many but also because they know that drugs used to treat psychosomatic disorders in people – problems like clinical anxiety or compulsive behaviour – work in dogs too.

By denying dogs, or any other animals for that matter, the 'human' ability of consciousness, people separate themselves from the rest of the living world. And once separated, the rest of the world can be treated differently. Dogs become expendable items of light relief, with financial rather than intrinsic value. The lower the financial value the more expendable the dog is, which is why random-bred dogs, or mongrels, are more likely to find themselves in dog shelters than purebreds.

22. A psychiatrist says it's easier for people to talk to me than to other people. Isn't that stupid?

Dogs are unambiguous compared to people. What you see is what you get. Dogs may be speechless but they are perfect communicators. Well over eighty per cent of dog owners feel their dogs understand their feelings and emotions. This curious fact has been lucidly examined among deaf people in Britain who acquired 'hearing dogs' to act as their ears, to tell them there is a knock on the door or a smoke alarm has gone off or the baby is crying – sounds that the hearing world takes for granted. In a study that lasted several years, the investigators observed that feelings of self esteem, self reliance and personal worth dramatically increased in people who acquired 'hearing dogs'. These improvements were far in excess of expectations. When the investigators studied these changes in more detail they observed that the deaf people and their dogs were actually communicating with each other, or at least the people felt they were. The communication was mute. No words or any other noises were exchanged, communication took place through body language. The deaf people felt that their dogs understood how they felt emotionally, without the need to explain. They felt their dogs understood better than people did; that with people they needed to explain things verbally but with dogs they did not. And because these people had living beings in their homes that understood their feelings and emotions, their feelings of self worth and confidence improved.

If this is the experience of deaf people it is very likely that hearing people experience similar emotional benefits just by saying, 'Isn't life rough, Ben?', and feeling that Ben does not have to respond. Ben understands fully and there is no need for him to respond. This is mute understanding at its purest. In reality, it may be that Ben has no inkling whatsoever about the emotional turmoil of his owner, but that does not matter. His owner feels that Ben understands and that is what is most important. The most popular branch of modern psychiatry is 'non-interventive', an approach that is similar in many ways to the non-judgemental, non-interventive approach dogs have to their owners' problems. If it really works, it is not only easier to talk to dogs, it's astoundingly cheaper and available twenty-four hours a day without appointment.

23. *I am a Yorkshire Terrier. I know I'm pretty but why is it I can get away with almost anything, including murder, but my scruffier friend can't?*

Physical attractiveness is intensely important to people. That is why piggy-eyed, scaly-tailed rats – intelligent, affectionate and very trainable animals – are despised, while innocent-eyed, sensuous but spiteful, moody, bloodthirsty cats are loved, treasured and admired.

People like attractive people. A handsome man accused of murder is more likely to be found not guilty than an un-attractive one. Disruptive behaviour by an attractive child is more likely to be excused by the teacher than disruptive be-haviour by an unattractive child. Physically attractive politi-cians are more likely to win elections than less attractive ones.

The same human attitude applies to dogs. Pure-bred dogs, bred for coat colour, length and texture, and for body shape and size, may have been bred at one time for practical pur-poses, but are almost universally bred today for what people feel are 'good looks'. Physical attributes, like a thick or wiry coat to protect the dog from the elements, are now selectively enhanced to appeal to people's eyes and sense of touch.

Really good-looking dogs can literally 'get away with murder' because of another human idiosyncrasy. Curiously, people don't particularly like absolute perfection in other people, or in dogs. They prefer perfection tinged with a little human weakness or, in the case of dogs, reversion to canine instincts. In one lovely scientific study an American psycholo-gist had actors answer an educational quiz. Several actors were asked to answer questions equally correctly, but one of the actors was asked to make a noisy commotion and say, in an anguished tone, 'Oh my goodness, I've spilled coffee all over my suit'. That was the person who listeners to tapes of the conversations found most attractive.

A seductively pretty Yorkshire Terrier is admired for its physical perfection. But when it chases and kills a cat, although its owner may be distressed, there is a deep-seated feeling of admiration because the dog has demonstrated that not only is it pretty, but it is still also a dog. If an ugly dog were to commit the same crime it would receive far less human consideration.

24. *I'm a fluffy Bichon Frisé. Why is he so embarrassed to be seen walking me?*

Dogs play several roles in people's lives. One of them is to act as an extension of the owner's personality. People like to project their own sexual image through the clothes they wear and dogs are, to some extent, accessories to that image. That is why, historically, men in general prefer either lean, muscular, short-coated dogs or working breeds, while women may select the same shapes but also choose more cuddly varieties like Bichons, Shih Tzus and Pekingese. There is still a class distinction among men in their choice of dogs. Working-class men tend to prefer guarding breeds such as German Shepherds, Dobermans and Rottweilers. If they must have a medium-sized dog it is usually a muscular Bull Terrier variety, a Staffordshire, English or Pit Bull Terrier. If a small dog is forced upon them they prefer hard 'teeth and muscles' dogs such as Jack Russell Terriers.

Middle-class man is different. He is usually university educated and is aware of his female as well as his male side. If he is confident in his sexual identity he is quite happy to be seem in public walking a ball of fluff, and may even take pride in the fact that he is associated with what is still to many people a feminine image. Of course, some men have no say in what the family dog looks like. In these circumstances, basic man might want a masculine-image dog but find himself lumbered with a Chihuahua. He will be much less embarrassed to walk this dog if, small as it is, the dog has a deep blood lust and tries to attack anything living.

25. *Why does she take me to the vet each time I wink? Is she compulsive?*

Definitely a worrier. Possibly an exaggerated motherer. And maybe she is not getting enough emotional nourishment anywhere else and is reciprocating in the only way she knows how. Other emotionally malnourished people become obsessive feeders, bloating their dogs with calories of love.

Some people, perfectly sensible when it comes to the health of their own children, do overreact when a dog is apparently unwell. If a child feels itchy or has diarrhoea or has vomited, parents take simple remedial action. But if a dog is scratching excessively, has the runs or vomits, it is taken to the vet immediately. One simple explanation is that people are better at understanding human medical complaints than they are at knowing what to do when their dog has the blues. They forget that the principles of care are exactly the same: prevent the problem from getting any worse; eliminate the cause; promote recovery and repair.

Natural born worriers will obtain professional advice just as quickly for their dogs as for their children. Obsessive and compulsive medical seekers are the same – so too are ardent motherers. The emotionally malnourished are different. These people use the dog as a ticket of admission to talk to the veterinarian, someone they see as compassionate and understanding; a good listener. The dog's problem may be trivial – an itchy bottom or waxy ears – but it provides a valid reason for an appointment. There is a degree of learned helplessness in this behaviour. The dog owner visits the vet and gets a personal emotional reward because the vet listens and appears to care. Now that the owner knows that this is available she will be even more willing to call the vet the next time her dog has the slightest change from normal. The behaviour is self rewarding and in that sense becomes compulsive.

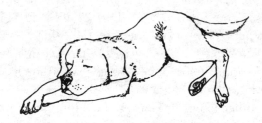

26. *People are strange. One day I'm the most important thing in their lives, the next I'm kicked out of the house. Why are people so inconsistent?*

People have ambivalent feelings about dogs. In one sense the pet dog is a true family member. It is fed, housed and cared for like other family members. It participates in family activities, from watching television to walking in parks to family holidays. People come to see their dogs as individuals, different from all others, even from others of the same breed. People who live with dogs eventually treat them as unique and irreplaceable individuals. They worry when their dogs are unwell and mourn when they die.

On the other hand, dogs are almost infinitely replaceable. In most countries there are always more dogs looking for homes than there are homes available for dogs. Dogs have a financial value and virtually anything with a finite value is replaceable. The legal definition of the dog clouds matters even more. In most cultures dogs are classified as 'chattels', items owned by people. Until recently, in court cases, dog owners have been awarded only the replacement value of a dog after it has died or been lost through negligence. Recently, some courts have modified their views and have also granted costs for 'loss of affection', but the general legal definition reinforces the concept that a dog is simply an item with a specific value.

The inconsistency in people's emotional attitude towards dogs is still based on the prevailing feeling that the human is a distinct and unique species, separate from all others. This attitude is a relic from cultural history. Changes are gradually taking place and the feeling of domination and control over all animals, including dogs, is being eroded and replaced by a feeling of responsibility towards other animals. In the near future, however, dogs will continue to lead threatened lives; loved one day, abandoned the next.

27. *I live with a dogaholic. Whenever she sees a stray dog she gets an impulsive desire to bring it home. Why?*

This can be simply the unalloyed care-giving response of natural nurturers, but it can also be the behaviour of people who find it difficult to communicate with other people and choose instead to surround themselves with animals. Although these people are reluctant to admit it, there is an element of power and control in their actions. They feel they cannot control their own or other people's lives, but in their chosen role of canine saviour all the rescued dogs owe their lives and well-being to their rescuer.

Taken to an extreme, animal collecting becomes an addiction. Addictions to 'negatives' such as drug taking or gambling are widely acknowledged, but people can also develop addictions to healthy and rewarding activities such as sexual activity or care-giving. In the context of rescuing dogs, these people fail to set limits to their behaviour and end up committing vast amounts of their time, energy and emotion to saving stray dogs.

This can become obsessive and uncontrollable. A point is reached where animal collecting replaces relationships with other people. There simply is no time for human relationships and, if there is time, there is no emotional energy left. Eventually, stray dogs replace intimate relations with people. Stray gatherers fulfil their need to be care-givers by investing all their time looking after lost dogs. Because the dogs are almost always willing to soak up this emotional Niagara, co-dependency develops. Dogs and carers need each other and this leads to the repetitive, obsessive behaviour typical of all addicts. Dog addicts usually deny they are addicted to rescuing strays. They say they can control their habit, but they can't. In extreme cases, they stop taking care of their own personal hygiene and invest all their energy in caring for their dogs. Breaking the habit is difficult, almost impossible, because of the powerful rewards and the constant supply of abandoned dogs that 'need them'.

Animal addiction is far more common in women than in men and develops independently of class or financial worth. Dog rescue centres are like honey pots to addicts. Detoxification and recovery is possible, but, as with all other potent addictions, difficult to complete. Relapses back into addiction are common.

28. *I am clean, healthy, well groomed and generally speaking I quite like humans. Why do some people take an instant dislike to me without even knowing what I'm like?*

Few people genuinely hate dogs – on average only about four per cent according to surveys in North America and Europe (over twenty per cent hate cats) – but when statistics are broken down further, there are significant differences according to where people live and their social background. The most likely person to hate dogs is an urban mother with more than five children who rents a high-rise flat from the local council, does not have a garden and has never had a dog. Over ten per cent of mothers in these circumstances 'dislike dogs very much'. At the other end of the spectrum, the individuals who like dogs the most are owner-occupiers of detached houses with gardens in open country, who have two resident children. In these circumstances, over eighty per cent like dogs.

Growing up with a dog is the most important reason for liking dogs and, unsurprisingly, being bitten by one is the most common reason for hating them. Hating dogs can be attributed to a number of other factors. Some human personalities are obsessed with hygiene and consider dogs 'unclean'. This may be a cultural vestige of the Judeo-Christian tradition, although it is actually most prevalent in Islamic cultures. It is also a characteristic of certain fastidious personalities regardless of their cultural background. Science calls these people anal-retentives. Others, either through cultural conditioning or innate feelings of superiority, profess a generalized dislike of all animals. Although small in numbers these people are exceedingly effective in broadcasting their dislikes.

29. *My owner dresses me in a thick leather harness covered with metal studs. He's named me Tyson. Why does he think this turns me into a weapon?*

He does not just *think* so. In the eyes of society it *does* turn a dog into a weapon. Regardless of whether a dog knows how to fight or not, other people will respond to the image the owner gives the dog and think of it as threatening. This can be deadly for dogs.

Bull Terriers and defence breeds like Rottweilers and Dobermans are most likely to be dressed to look like Hell's Angels' mascots. But that alone does not make an efficient fighter. Lack of obedience training, or intentional attack training does. This is more likely to be the fate of dogs that live with men between the ages of eighteen and thirty in urban working-class homes. In the United States, if a dog is an American Pit Bull Terrier and it has been used for fighting, there is more than a fifty per cent likelihood that its male owner already has a criminal record for violence.

In Britain and some other countries, certain breeds of dog have been accused – and convicted – of being dangerous weapons, regardless of their parentage or ownership. This is a consequence of human emotional hysteria and has little to do with canine behavioural reality. The American Pit Bull Terrier, Japanese Tosa and Dogo Argentino are three such breeds. These and many other breeds are descended from dogs used in bull baiting or dog fighting, but genetics alone does not create a weapon. Other breeds such as the Rottweiler, Doberman and German Shepherd also stand accused of being weapons but, according to medical statistics and veterinary surveys, these breeds are no more likely than the average dog to bite.

Human vanities and aspirations – men and women wanting a dog to look like a weapon, dressing it aggressively, amputating its ears to make it look fiercer – these are the root cause of the problem. People use dogs as projections of their true personalities or, more often, as a projection of the way they would like to be perceived. The problem is not with dogs. It is with their owners.

30. *Will people get upset when I die?*

Dogs get upset when dogs die and people do too. Dogs are honest about their feelings. When dog friends die, almost half of all dogs – forty-six per cent – suffer from a decreased appetite. Forty-three per cent lose their confidence. Thirty-nine per cent sleep more. Thirty per cent bark more, while thirty-four per cent bark less. Well over half – sixty-one per cent – seek out and ask for more attention and affection from people.

Most dog owners also get deeply upset when their dog dies although some, men in particular, try to hide their feelings. The death of a dog combines the loss of companionship, the interruption of routine and, in a curious way, the loss of innocence. All of these losses are very distressing.

People experience the same feelings of loss when their dogs die as they do when close friends and relatives die. They may deny that the death has happened, get angry with themselves, their family or their veterinarian for allowing the death to occur, feel deep, inconsolable grief or the need to be alone, or demand constant emotional support. Life changes significantly. Some people find it difficult to concentrate – so difficult they cannot work. Eventually, with time, the loss becomes accepted and integrated into the cumulative experiences of life. In that sense the death has been a learning experience and the owner is able to reconstruct his or her life in the absence of the dog.

This process lasts for a varying length of time but on average it takes almost a year to complete. It is significantly different from the way people grieve when young friends and relatives die only in one aspect: when dogs die there is little grieving for 'what might have been', one of the most potent aspects of the grief felt when children die.

Grieving may begin even before a dog dies, as soon as the veterinarian gives the 'bad news'. Once a person knows that their dog is terminally ill, that person's social life changes. It is not unusual for him or her to cancel engagements, work less efficiently, avoid holidays and concentrate all emotional energy on the dog. This is most likely to occur in people who have made a major emotional investment in their dog, perhaps because of a lack of contact, involvement and support from other people. In these circumstances, people are not only upset, they may be depressed, stop eating, find it difficult to speak to other people and find themselves incapable of coping with even minor responsibilities. This form of grieving is not unusual in compulsive care-givers. According to John Bowlby, the psychologist who first described the vast importance of 'attachment', the compulsive care-giver satisfies his or her need for attachment by becoming a permanent 'giver' rather than a 'receiver'. He says, 'The person who develops in this way has found that the only bond of affection available is one in which he must always be the care-giver, and that the only care he can ever receive is the care he gives.' This is the personality type that suffers most when a companion dog dies.

Many dog owners, but especially those who buy books about the way their dogs or they themselves behave, have made a significant emotional investment in their canine relationships. The loss, or even the anticipated loss of their dog, can create complicated, often prolonged reactions. This is a recognized phenomenon and organizations exist throughout North America, Europe and Japan to offer support to grieving dog owners.

31. *Will my death really be a 'rite of passage' for the kids in my family?*

The death of a pet is not only a 'rite of passage' for children; in its own way each death is a milestone in adult lives too.

The Canadian naturalist and author Farley Mowat wrote about the death of his dog: 'I did not know that, in its passing, it had made an end to the best years that I had lived'. Mowat did not mean that his relationship with his dog really made for the best years of his life. Like so many other dog owners he unknowingly divided his life into ten- to twelve-year segments that happened to coincide with the life spans of a series of dogs.

Many people, when they think back to childhood, adolescence and early adulthood, find themselves dividing their lives into 'dog' units. I do the same. The first part of my life was the 'Sparkie' period. My teens became the 'Misty' and 'Duchess' period. I had no dog in my twenties but my thirties was the 'Honey' period and my forties the 'Liberty' and 'Lexington' period. Of course, I don't actively think of my dogs first when I recall these stages of my life but rather, unwittingly, I use the dogs to define the beginning and end of each period. The writer Gail Sheehy uses the term 'passages' to define these sections of life.

My dog 'Sparkie's death, when I was ten years old, was a 'rite of passage' in that hers was the first close death I experienced. Relatives had died but never before someone or something I lived with, played with, tickled, fed, comforted or sought comfort from. Symbolically, the dog's death was my loss of innocence, of childhood 'animal' innocence. In a peculiar way the dog's death was a 'rite of passage' from the 'natural' life of childhood to the 'cultural' life of adulthood.

In the same sense Farley Mowat's loss of his dog when Mowat was in his thirties was, only in retrospect, his 'rite of passage' from the 'best years of his existence' on to the next phase of his life.

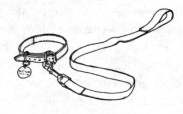

32. *Why do people get embarrassed about their emotions when dogs die?*

This is a unique aspect of the grieving process people experience when dogs die. Over seventy-five per cent of dog owners
are 'deeply distraught' when their dog dies, but Western cultures have no accepted ways of coping with these feelings.
The death of a close fellow human is an 'earth stopper' and in
response each culture or society has developed rituals and
customs to ease the pain. In virtually every world civilization,
a human death leads to open and genuine support from
others. Immediately following a death there is increased activity and communication. Emotional barriers come down.
Friends and relatives are less inhibited than they usually are.
There is more physical contact, more touching. And, of
course, there is ceremony and ritual.

When a dog dies, the response is almost the complete reverse. Western religions – Judaism, Christianity and Islam –
offer no rituals or ceremonies. (In contrast, Buddhism, Hindu-
ism and more obscure but equally ancient Eastern religions
such as Zoroastrianism, have time honoured rituals that accompany animal death.) Activity decreases, if only because
the dog-generated activities of feeding, exercising and playing
are no longer available. The emotional barriers that come
down when people die remain, or are even raised higher,
when a dog dies. Visitors are less likely to call because they are
embarrassed about how to behave. Instead of letters, flowers
and phone calls people experience greater isolation and lone-
liness. Within the family there may be less communication
than normal. Routines are expected to continue as if nothing
has happened.

Western cultures stipulate that the death of a dog should

not even cause a hiccough in the flow of life. Yet those people who were close to the dog *know* how deeply they feel the loss and it is this dichotomy that leads to embarrassment. 'How can I feel such emotional desolation over the death of my dog when I did not feel as bad when my relative died?', they ask themselves. Western religions have only recently begun to acknowledge these feelings and create rituals for pet loss. The newest Western 'religion', Animal Rights, has the most advanced programme to help people cope with the death of their pets.

33. Why do people care more for homeless dogs than homeless people?

Once again, innocence is a key factor. The dog is a man-made creation, although it is also true that dogs are in part self domesticated. Between 10,000 and 15,000 years ago Asian wolves were attracted to sites of permanent human habitation. In this new ecological habitat, survival of the fittest was responsible for the reduction in tooth and body size and for increased 'tameabililty'. A point was reached when dog breeding came under the control of people; from then on the dog was 'domesticated'. In virtually all its varied forms the dog now depends upon people for its survival, just as children do. Domestication, some people say, robbed the dog of the means by which it could take care of itself. That is why some people feel a personal responsibility for any stray or homeless dog.

There is a little theoretical mumbo jumbo in this hypothesis. Not all homeless dogs are innocents; wandering offers a vicarious thrill to many, males in particular. Permanent wandering leads to selective survival and produces distinctive minds and bodies. The Australian Dingo, New Guinea Singing Dog, perhaps even the Israeli Canaan Dog and State of Georgia Carolina Dog are examples.

Homeless people do not provoke a similar response because not all of them share the image of innocence that dogs have. Those who are homeless through their own innocence are grouped together with those who are homeless through drug or alcohol abuse or, as is the case with some adolescents, for the excitement of living rough and snubbing the accepted precepts of their society. This latter group shares strong similarities with some stray young male dogs, but many animal lovers fail to recognize this.

CHAPTER THREE

The Secret Foibles of Dog Owners

34. *Very soon after I was born, before I could really do anything about it, they cut my tail off! Why did they do that? Is there any religious significance?*

Amputating tails is done simply to satisfy the needs of fashion. People will tie themselves in knots to justify their reasons for doing so but when it comes down to reality, it is a European tradition started several thousand years ago through superstition and perpetuated today by human rather than canine interests. Yes, it does have a religious significance, if you include witchcraft and hocus pocus in your definition of religion.

Tail cutters defend their tradition by saying it doesn't hurt. It does. It hurts as much as it would hurt to twist off the smallest finger of human new-born babies without anaesthetic. The skin, bone, muscles and nerve supply are about the same. People who believe in tail docking say it doesn't hurt because the pup does not cry out until after the amputation is well under way or has been completed. This is only because pain transmission is so slow. In adults, the feeling of pain travels to the brain at 120 metres per second. At birth it is 60 times slower.

Some people believe that dogs are healthier without tails. There is not the slightest piece of evidence to suggest this is true. Indeed, there is compelling evidence to suggest that dogs that have had their tails amputated, Boxer dogs in particular, have a higher incidence of lower-back pain than those with tails. A tail is built to wag at a healthy speed. The fast metronome motion of a stump places excessive strain on the lower back, causing inflammation and eventual arthritic changes in the back bones.

57

The origins of tail amputation can be traced to Europe's oldest natural history book, written by the Roman, Pliny the Elder. In *Naturalis Historia*, Pliny describes the Spaniard Columella's way of preventing rabies in dogs: 'If, forty days after being whelped, the dog's tail is docked and the end bitten off, the tail does not grow again and the dog is not liable to madness.' Within living memory, in Yorkshire, some pups still had their tails bitten off by their keepers.

Some countries have banned tail docking as a needless mutilation. Others contemplate doing so. As long as some dog breeders react by knee-jerk reflex rather than through thoughtful consideration, dogs will continue needlessly to lose what is, to them, an extremely useful appendage.

35. *Will they ever eat me? Is it a cultural thing?*

This depends upon where a dog lives. Yes, it is a 'cultural thing' but its origins are nutritional rather than strictly cultural.

The dog has served as an emergency source of food in most regions of the world. Herbivores – vegetable eaters – are the best meat source because they convert vegetation to meat. Meat eaters, like dogs, are very inefficient because they must eat meat to make meat. That is the main reason why dog is not on many menus.

Dog meat has been eaten at one time or another throughout Europe, Africa, Asia and the Americas but only as a response to starvation. It is still eaten in response to hunger, as Russian soldiers found themselves doing during the war in Chechnia. Only in Polynesia, China and Korea did eating dog pass from need into culture.

In these regions of the world, dogs were selectively bred for food. Some of these 'edible' dogs still exist as distinct breeds, for example the Hawaiian Poi Dog, the Chinese Chow Chow and the Korean Jindo. Dogs are reasonably safe today in most parts of Polynesia but still at risk from the stew pot in China and especially Korea, where many are available for culinary purposes. The Chinese government and, to a greater extent, the Korean government have tried to ban restaurants serving dog meat but this has only succeeded in driving the restaurants away from the parts of those countries visited by Western tourists. (Japanese dogs, incidentally, never had to avoid Japanese kitchens. Until the 1860s, no land living mammal – carnivore or herbivore – was eaten in that country, although in rural regions hunting deer with dogs actually took place. To justify eating the catch, animals were given odd names. Wild boar, for example, was called 'whale of the woods'.) As Korea and the cities of China adopt Western cultural values, pet dogs are increasingly valued more for their companionship than for their taste. Eating dog meat will diminish as the social and financial value of dogs increases.

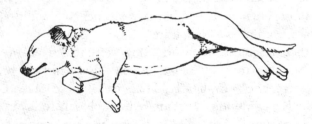

36. *Why have I been injected with a microchip. Isn't this Big Brother tactics?*

Dogs are the guinea pigs in an identification exercise that may well involve their owners in the future. Here is the picture. Identifying lost, stray or stolen dogs can be difficult as many dogs look similar to each other. If a dog loses its collar and name tag and if it does not have a tattoo number, its chances of being positively identified are left to luck.

In response, manufacturers have invented a small, inert glass capsule, the size of a rice grain, that includes an information carrying transponder. This 'rice grain' of information is injected just under the skin of a dog's neck where it rests permanently, without migrating elsewhere. Because it is glass and inert the dog's body does not react to it. It does not bother the dog and the information in the transponder is 'read' simply by passing a 'reader' over the dog's body. If there is a transponder under the dog's skin, the 'reader' finds it and prints out the information.

Microchips are cheap, easy to install, non-irritating and permanent. Dog owners feel more secure knowing their dogs carry permanent identification that is virtually impossible to tamper with. Government Departments and Ministries of Agriculture are so impressed that in Japan, Europe and North America systems are being developed to insert microchips into all livestock and use them to track animal movements from farm to farm and eventually to abattoirs. Yes, there is an element of Orwell's Big Brother watching, but the system does ensure that potential disease problems can be tracked. At the same time it could eliminate financial hanky-panky, a common phenomenon in the world of agricultural subsidies.

Initially, microchips were developed to identify dogs and, to a lesser extent, cats. Then agricultural animals were included. Now, there is a possibility that people will be added to the list. Some individuals in government departments are simply thrilled with the idea of permanently identifying the human population they deal with. They argue that by doing so, in case of injury and unconsciousness, all that is needed to determine identity is a microchip reader. Any specific conditions or problems such as diabetes or drug allergies would also be instantly known. With a permanent tracking system implanted in people, government agencies could carry 'consumer use' taxation policies to their logical conclusion, for example charging for time spent on roads or using street lights. Microchips benignly benefit dogs because they make identification so much easier, but in the wrong hands they could be a serious hazard to dogs' owners.

37. *I've got cousins in both Europe and North America that have been bred, intentionally, with wolves. What's the value?*

There is a certain type of human personality, usually male but not necessarily so, that dreams of returning dogs to their origins by adding healthy wolf to degenerate dog. These people are usually between eighteen and thirty-five. They may have tattoos. They wear shell suits.

In the recent past there have been distinct cultural episodes during which dogs were bred with wolves. The first this century started with seemingly altruistic intentions. In the 1920s a Dutch dog breeder introduced wolf blood into his German Shepherds in an attempt to increase resistance to canine distemper, at that time the most common lethal infection afflicting dogs. The breeder, Leendert Saarloos, lost his ethical high ground when most of the first litter actually died of distemper. Wolf blood did not improve disease resistance in dogs but Saarloos kept breeding, producing the breed now known as the Saarloos Wolfhound or Wolf Dog.

In the 1960s, in California, the emerging hippy culture replicated what Saarloos did, but in an anarchic way appropriate to the times. Zuni, Hopi and other south-eastern native peoples' stories and customs featured prominently in hippy culture. Many of these stories involved the constancy, integrity and fidelity of the wolf. In a classic attempt at a 'return to nature', dogs were bred with wolves but not in an organized way. The descendants either died off or the new wolf genes became diluted through their descendants' successive breedings with other dogs.

At the same time, Czechoslovak breeders were breeding dogs with wolves, but with a specific purpose. Veterinarians at

Brno University were interested in enhancing the German Shepherd's guarding ability. They crossed Shepherds with Carpathian wolves. The results were timid animals, often fearful of strangers and needing intense patience on the part of their handlers to be trained properly. Here, too, the experiment was an obvious failure from the beginning but the results of these matings live on as the breed known as the Czech Wolf Dog.

There is no value in breeding dogs with wolves, but it is a great ego trip for the breeders. It continues to be an aspiration of many, especially German Shepherd and Nordic dog owners.

38. *I've got dignity. I've got bearing. If you ask me I'm pretty majestic. I'm a smart, muscular guy. Why am I clipped in such a demeaning fashion with puffballs of fur on my legs and tail?*

Another human foible. People use dogs as helpers and companions, but they also use dogs as emblems, totems, ornaments and status symbols. People clip dogs in funny ways for their own vain reasons, although this form of canine topiary does have distant and practical origins.

Some popular breeds descend from mountain dogs – ancient breeds selectively bred for dense, matted or 'corded' coats that offered protection during fights with wolves. Guarding breeds like Hungarian Pulis and Kommondors still have protective corded coats. Other breeds such as Standard Poodles and Portuguese Water Dogs are probably descendants of these mountain dogs, but hundreds of years ago they branched out into a new activity: retrieving arrows from water.

This was a useful activity both in war and peace for soldiers or hunters. Selective breeding enhanced the dog's desire and ability to retrieve from water, but a dense coat was both a hindrance and an advantage. Thick fur offered insulation but it also made swimming more difficult. To make dogs more efficient swimmers, hunters clipped the hair from the legs, leaving it thick only over the vulnerable joints. They left a full coat over the chest and belly, to protect the internal organs from thermal shock, but clipped close over the powerful thighs and hips. Finally, they clipped their dog's tails, leaving only a puff at the tip to help the tail float.

In Spain and Portugal, dogs graduated from arrow retrieval

to fishermen's companion, swimming from boat to boat as message bearers and helping to pull nets in by swimming to cork floats and returning them to their masters. Some water dogs still perform these functions today in the Iberian peninsula and have their coats cut accordingly.

Standard Poodles (the French name, *Caniche*, means 'duck dog' and describes its former practical role) are rarely used for utilitarian purposes, although the breed's size, responsiveness and sensibility combine to make it an impressively capable worker. Instead, many are clipped like box hedges in an ornamental garden. This pleases their owners, but few others, as it robs the breed of its natural and deserved dignity.

39. *Why am I not allowed in the nursery? All I want to do is have a good look and sniff.*

Some people fear that their dog is dangerous to their new child. One hideous fantasy has the dog cuddling up so closely to the new baby that the baby gets smothered. Another has the dog, in a fit of jealous pique, attacking and killing the baby. Both worries are unjustified, although dogs should never be left unattended with babies or young children.

The smothering scenario requires the dog to get into the baby's crib – impossible for most dogs. The jealousy scenario is a human worry with a little more justification. Dogs are selfish, they love attention and don't like to see others getting it. If a dog has been a 'child substitute', a stopgap until a couple have a child of their own, it is very likely that it has come to enjoy its primogeniture. A human baby getting what was previously the dog's attention is a threat and a dog may attack the baby as a way of reminding the parents that it was there first.

This is easily avoided, but not by preventing a dog from looking and sniffing in the nursery. A good sniff satisfies a dog's need to know. Sniffing for a dog is like reading a newspaper. All sorts of information is imparted in smells. At the same time, people should avoid sudden changes in canine routine; eating, playing and sleeping should follow old patterns.

People should anticipate that both emotionally and physically they will be sucked dry after a baby arrives in their home and should alter a dog's routines before the baby's arrival so that the dog does not combine one and one and produce a genuine two.

40. *I look around at other dogs and all I see is fat, fat, fat. Why are so many of my canine friends getting fatter?*

It's not just because dog food tastes so much better than it once did. And it's not just because people are busier and have less time to exercise their dogs. The number of fat dogs will continue to rise because of human demographics and emotions.

Veterinarians estimate that at least one third of all dogs are clinically overweight. Pet food manufacturers realize that this makes for an excellent market and have responded to the epidemic of canine obesity by producing a vast range of low calorie tinned and dry foods. Even low calorie snack foods are available, usually called 'light', as if a feathery name vaporizes fat.

Fat dogs are wholly a human creation and their perpetuation lies in the hidden role dogs play in many people's lives. In any family that houses an overweight canine, the dog has discovered the soft touch, the person who is most likely to give it treats. More often than not this is a male, usually the silverback male – the family breadwinner. The dog discovers that although the woman and children in the family follow the vet's instructions, cut down calories and increase activity, the dominant male is, curiously, the weak link. He gives the dog extra food because he finds it difficult to show his emotions, to be physical, to touch. He doesn't do these things with his family. With his children, he expresses his affection by giving them money, but with his dog he offers biscuits and snacks.

Dogs quickly learn who these people are and manipulate them. That is why the level of obesity in the dog population remains large, but in the future it will increase for other reasons.

Most developed countries have ageing populations. In Europe, North America, Japan and Australasia the elderly – over sixty years old – are the fastest growing part of the population. Dog ownership is lowest among people over sixty, which is why the dog population will continue to drop. Dogs will get smaller because older people prefer small dogs. They will get plumper, not because the elderly are less capable of providing exercise but because they are the most responsible sector of society. The elderly are more likely to neuter their dogs and neutered dogs have a greater tendency to go to fat. In years to come dogs will be fewer in number, smaller and fatter.

41. *In my grandfather's time, dogs died from infections or diseases. Now it seems like I'm more likely to inherit my medical problems from my parents. Why are inherited diseases seemingly so more common today? I know people have something to do with it.*

People are responsible for virtually all the health changes in the dog population, both good and bad. On the good side, previously common and lethal infectious diseases such as distemper, viral hepatitis and leptospirosis have been banished through effective vaccination programmes, although all of these infections still occur regionally. The immediate consequence is that dogs live longer and this makes them more likely to suffer from inherited conditions later in life.

On the negative side, there has been an insidious increase in the incidence of inherited disease. Some of these diseases, like valvular heart disease in Cavalier King Charles Spaniels, shorten dogs' lives. Others, such as hereditary joint conditions or blindness, make life painful or physically difficult.

People breed dogs for their looks and personalities. Those with the best looks and personalities are the most likely to be permitted to continue breeding. The very best looking become industrial strength breeders and can father hundreds of young. While this practice might pass on a dog's good looks, it is just as likely to concentrate deleterious conditions in his descendants. These 'bad' but hidden genes are responsible for inherited diseases. When dogs bred randomly, inherited disease was less common, but as the dog's gene pool has shrunk to about 400 breeds, bad genes have become concentrated in about 400 different populations.

People will continue to breed dogs selectively because individual breeds are now so important. Guide Dogs for the Blind, in Britain, found a possible solution to the problem of inherited diseases, specifically eye problems in Labradors. They simply crossed Labradors with Golden Retrievers, diluting the dangerous gene pool while at the same time perpetuating the personality needed for the dogs to act as eyes for blind people. A little more canine miscegenation can only be a good thing. Cockerpoos and Labradoodles are less likely to suffer from inherited medical problems than the purebred populations they come from.

42. *If I were a purebred dog rather than a mongrel would people take better care of me?*

Unfortunately, yes. People value purebred dogs over mongrels and it shows in dog shelter statistics. Purebred dogs are just as likely to stray from home but are much less likely to be surrendered to a dog shelter.

Purebred dogs have a specific replacement value while, until recently, mongrels had little or no value at all. Sensible dog shelter administrators realized that by giving away dogs for free they were perpetuating the idea that these dogs were worthless. Good shelters now charge reasonable fees for their dogs, not just to bring needed money into the charities but also to underline the fact that the dogs are genuinely valued.

43. *I am a big, handsome German Shepherd. I enjoy guarding the house. My name is Benjamin but I'm called everything from Ben to Benjie. Why do I have so many names?*

People get a variety of rewards from their dogs. A dog's name is a clue to what people emotionally want from a dog and in that respect I am no different from other dog owners. Like Benjamin, my dogs have a variety of names, each used in its specific context.

My dogs Liberty and Lexington are called by those names, or Lib and Lex, or Libby and Lexy. I have heard my daughter call Liberty Libbywibby. My son usually calls her Libs.

Originally, I chose names that are not given to human children because I wanted to make a statement. I was saying that my dogs are not child substitutes but rather, uniquely, *dog*. In doing so I was going against the trend. Increasingly, dogs are being given human names. For example, in Britain, Ben and Sally are extremely popular. So too are Sam, Sheba, Cindy, Max, Susie, Penny and Toby. Names like Rover and Rex are extremely uncommon.

Full names like Benjamin, Liberty and Lexington give dignity to dogs. Owners use these names when they expect their dogs to respond smartly or intelligently, or when proudly introducing their dogs to other people. When an owner uses a strong, full name, a point is made. The owner may genuinely respect the dog but certainly wants it to be respected.

Monosyllabic names like Ben, Lib and Lex are used more informally, especially during training. Most dog owners know, or soon learn, that dogs respond best to distinctive, single syllable names. Unwittingly, people shorten long, pretentious names like my dogs have to shorter, more practical ones.

In English, adding a 'y' or 'ie' to a name makes it feminine. Bennie or Benjie, Libby and Lexy all are soft names. Their use infers gentleness of spirit. When a dog's name is softened in this way, owners are saying symbolically that their dogs are trustworthy and reliable. Some people specify an exact and distinct spelling for a dog's name: for example Ben-Gee or Lybie or Lecksea. It is most likely these dogs are more important than average for their owners, either as status symbols or as emotional supports.

Finally, there are nicknames or love names. Psychologists call these 'release' names. Libbywibby is such a name but it is just as likely that people will use completely different names in certain circumstances. 'Come on, Treasure, let's go to the park', 'Hello, Beautiful', 'Good morning, Sunshine' – these are names that parents or lovers use with intimates. Men use these affectionate names less frequently than women but they, too, have unique ways to express verbally their bonding with dogs. When my son calls our dog Libs, he is saying that the dog is an honorary member of a male brotherhood, and is inviting it to do male-bonding things like catch frisbees or jog together.

44. *They felt good to me and looked good to other dogs. Why were my ears amputated?*

There was a time when dogs were bred to 'bait' bulls; to bite them and chew them before slaughter, an ancient method of meat tenderizing. This evolved into a spectator sport where dogs were bred and trained to attack bulls simply for the mindless pleasure of people. In turn, this lead to dogs being selectively bred and trained to fight with each other. Because ears are easily damaged in fights, owners of fighting dogs sliced the ears off. This was a painful but practical way to reduce injuries during fights.

In the nineteenth century, in Germany in particular, a breathtaking variety of new breeds emerged including Dobermans, Schnauzers, Boxers and Great Danes. None of these breeds were bred for dog fighting but most of their original breeders came from military backgrounds. These men liked dogs that looked like weapons so they amputated their dogs' ears to make them look more like fierce fighters. Later on, as veterinary medicine developed into a modern medical science, veterinarians perpetuated the desired look, but more humanely, with anaesthetics and surgery.

The only reasons vets carry out these unpleasant amputations today is for the vanity of people and for financial reward. Cutting off the ears serves no purpose whatsoever for dogs. Indeed, if this operation were carried out for medical reasons, breeds like Cocker Spaniels would have their ears amputated, rather than Great Danes and Boxers.

In some countries, Britain for example, ears have not been amputated for over sixty years. Regrettably, this mutilation is still common today in the United States, Japan and Russia.

45. *Why does she think I love her more than her husband does?*

People feel that a dog's love is unconditional, pure and everlasting. The life-long 'puppy' in dogs – the licking and nuzzling, the pleasure sounds, the joyous body language – all of these create a feeling of unquestioning devotion, an absence of judging, total trust, unspoken understanding, boundless adoration and love.

The pet dog's apparent love and affection is 'super-abundant', greater than is possible in any adult human relationship and fills a subconscious void in people's lives. A husband can love just as deeply but is no competition for this fantasy.

46. *Why do they hate cats but love me? After all, both of us are simply successful carnivores who enjoy the company of humans.*

This human foible is part intuitive but also part cultural. In human evolution, people lived without domesticated animals for the first 99.7 per cent of their existence. Between 10,000 and 15,000 years ago, the greatest cultural change that ever affected humans occurred. Men willingly reduced the time they spent hunting and killing individual animals and increased the time spent caring for groups of animals and killing them selectively. Dogs were already there to assist herd management. After all, the wolf's social behaviour had programmed it for domestication, to work with people. Dogs were and still are useful. They might want to share in the meat but they willingly eat bits that people don't want and act as resident sanitary engineers, tidying the human settlement.

Cats never shared this close relationship with people. Although the Egyptians trained cheetahs to assist in the hunt, generally speaking cats were unwanted visitors in human settlements. Big cats were downright dangerous, while smaller cats killed small domestic animals like newborn piglets or lambs. People put up with cats only because they reduced vermin in granaries. Until very recently cats were solitary hunters; aloof, independent carnivores quite unlike willingly submissive dogs. Intuitively, people were drawn to the dog's social behaviour but not to the cat's seeming selfishness. Even today more people instinctively understand dogs than cats. Many find cats quite mysterious. Mystery can be attractive but this is appealing to fewer people than understanding.

Attraction to dogs and antipathy to cats is also cultural.

This dichotomy is most obvious in the differences between Christian and Islamic attitudes to dogs and cats. In Christian countries dogs are more likely to be revered and cats hated. In Islamic countries the reverse is true. This is because early Christians associated cats with devil worship, and in Europe the cat has suffered unfairly ever since. Early in the history of Islam, Moslems conquered Persia, obliterating the dominant dog-loving Zoroastrian religion and driving survivors into India. Just as the ancient Hebrews made idolatry, the religion of the Egyptians, the most potent of sins, so too the early Moslems turned the dog, an image of Zoroastrianism, into a cultural taboo. With the dog relegated to the cultural sidelines, the cat moved up several notches in its respect in Islamic countries, but, even so, a bedrock number of people in these countries still have an innate feeling of unease in the presence of cats.

47. *All I do is sit there looking blank. Why do they think I understand human language so well?*

The dog has sensitive hearing and in a surprisingly short period of time, sometimes in as little as a few minutes, learns to respond to human language. It learns what to do when it hears certain words – SIT – STAY – DOWN – EAT – GO – PARK. It associates these sounds with ideas. That does not mean that dogs understand the concept of language the way people do.

For example, people sometimes toilet train pups by saying 'HURRY UP' as the pup urinates or defecates. As an adult, a dog genuinely 'hurries up' when it hears those words spoken. But that does not mean that it understands what the words actually mean. A dog learns to associate those words with dumping urine or faeces just as Pavlov's dogs learned to dribble saliva when they heard bells because a bell was rung just before they were fed.

Dogs are very good at associating sounds that humans make with specific responses like car rides or lying down or giving a paw. That does not mean they understand language, yet because of this *apparent* understanding of language people willingly talk to dogs the way they talk to other people. That is because people find it difficult, almost impossible, to think like dogs. People often use conditional statements when talking to their dogs, or use past or future tenses: 'If you bark once more, you will get no supper', 'I will be back soon', 'Why did you do that?'. When people utter these sentences they really do think that dogs understand them. And because a dog is so well mannered, like the politest Japanese person not wishing to offend, it sits there, wide-eyed and intent, soaking up each uttered word, looking like it understands everything.

48. *I am brushed daily. I am whisked off to the pet parlour on a monthly basis for a short back and sides. I am fed the tastiest and most expensive of dog foods. I wear clothes from the best department stores. In many ways I am much like my owner. Does she think I am just a furry extension of her own personality?*

Perhaps. Most dogs are manifestations of their owner's personalities and some are simply fashion accessories.

A dog is most likely to become a fashion accessory either if it is unique or is already an icon of a specific human culture. Unique breeds enjoy 'flavour-of-the-month' status. The Shar Pei, the Chinese 'wrinkle dog', is a classic fashion accessory. It is a walking medical encyclopaedia of problems – skin allergies, eye and ear irritations, toe inflammations – yet it remains popular as a way for people to tell other people how unique they are. Getting a flavour-of-the-month dog is a method people use to say they are on the cutting edge of culture. Hairdressers love Shar Peis.

Even more common is the cultural statement made by specific breeds. Working-class Russians relish Black Russian Terriers, wiry hulks of nationalistic muscle. The Russian mafia prefer Moscow Watchdogs, up to 100 kilograms of thug, while their molls demand expensive Western toy breeds like Yorkshire Terriers.

Affluent Western European country people do not dress themselves up with thugs, or louche Afghans for that matter. They wear Labradors, Springer Spaniels or bloodthirsty Terriers. These breeds imply that their owners are 'of the land'. European royalty most frequently wear Labradors, Golden

Retrievers and Jack Russell Terriers, although Dachshunds and Cocker Spaniels also are popular.

People choose specific breeds to fit their own fashion image. In the 1980s, when the environmental movement and interest in animal welfare became mainstream, a significant shift in fashion accessories occurred. For the first time, random-bred or mongrel dogs became serious fashion statements. Environmentalists and animal welfarists found a philosophical contradiction in owning a pedigree dog and supporting their cause. The fashions conflicted. This was extremely good news for mutts. Since it coincided with an increase in interest in purebred dogs among working-class families, always the greatest resource for mutts, and as environmentalists and animal welfarists are less likely to let their dogs roam at will, the number of abandoned random-breds has dropped substantially during the last decade.

49. What's the difference between dog people and people who don't own dogs?

The greatest difference, perhaps the only real difference, is that dog people spent their childhoods with dogs. That is the most important predictor of whether people will acquire dogs. When you look at major aspects of personality, things like dominance, aggression, affiliation, sense of order, nurturing need or succorance, there is little, if anything, that separates these two groups.

Among dogs owners, however, there *are* differences in personalities and these are revealed by the type of dogs they like. The American Kennel Club classifies all dogs into the following groups: toys, terriers, hounds (sight and scent hunters), herders (livestock drivers and protectors), workers (large guarding breeds), sporting dogs (gun dogs) and non-sporting dogs (anything left over).

Of those people who own dogs, toy breed owners are the most nurturing and least dominant. Terrier owners are the least aggressive but most dependent on others for emotional support. Hound people are the friendliest. Herding breed owners are the most aggressive and orderly of all dog owners. Working breed people are the most dominant dog owners. Sporting breed owners are the wealthiest. Non-sporting breed owners are a mixed bag. In other words, it is easier to predict a person's personality according to the type of dog that person owns rather than by whether or not he or she has a dog.

50. *Why don't people understand how I know they are going on holiday?*

Once more, it is a case of people failing to understand that spoken language is not the only method of accurate communication.

Verbal language is what differentiates people from other animals. It is the human's particularly unique ability but other species of animals, including dogs, have equally unique but different abilities. The cognitive scientist Steven Pinker was at his wittiest when he said, 'We are simply a species of primate with our own act in nature's talent show, a knack for communicating information about who did what to whom by modulating the sounds we make when we exhale'.

People are so efficient at doing this that they feel it is the only possible way to communicate information accurately. They forget that their closest relatives, other primates like chimpanzees, are 'pre-verbal' yet are still able to communicate efficiently. In the 1970s and 1980s, sign-language experiments with chimps showed that their capacity to understand sign language is refined and sophisticated, so much so that chimps were able to make up accurate sign-language words to describe new objects or desires.

Sign language is simply a sophisticated development from body language, the most common method by which dogs communicate with each other from a distance. Dogs understand other dogs by watching them. They understand what people intend to do because people also use ritualized body language both to express emotion and to commit themselves to physical movements. This latter aspect of body language is collectively called 'intention movements'. By evolutionary coincidence the emotional body language and intention movements of dogs and people are similar. Because verbal language is such a profoundly effective aspect of the biological make-up of people's brains, it has replaced these two physical aspects of communication between individuals. People forget that physical communication can be equally effective in giving information. Dogs read the intention movements and emotional body signals unwittingly given out by people and know that a change is in the air.

51. *Why does Hollywood treat me so well?*

Hollywood understands that people are attracted to dogs for emotional reasons. The dog personifies loyalty, constancy, reliability and devotion. It is a best buddy, always there to help. Against overwhelming odds, dogs possess, as Lord Byron wrote in his epitaph to his dog, 'Beauty without vanity, strength without insolence, courage without ferocity'. Byron did not know it but he was really writing the job description for a Hollywood film star – male variety.

Hollywood likes dogs because dogs sell seats in cinemas. But there is more. In cartoons like *Lady and the Tramp* or *101 Dalmatians*, dogs portray sex stereotypes in crisp outline. Lady is soft, sensuous, curvy, cuddly and has outrageously long eyelashes. Tramp is sinewy, cocky, strutting and cool. He is street smart but, come fatherhood, becomes a perfect dad: cocky, cool but now caring too.

There was a time when Hollywood relegated dogs to children's films and tear-jerkers but, more recently, Hollywood realized that dogs are perfect buddies for fellas. In films, grown-up men like the actors Tom Hanks and Bill Murray, spend their lives with dogs. Hollywood's subliminal message is that the child remains alive in these men and Hollywood knows that this is a powerfully potent medicine for women.

52. *Is that why people use me in so many advertisements?*

Advertisers use dogs for a greater variety of reasons than Hollywood. After all, the dog has all the intrinsic values of the good salesman. In people's eyes it has empathy, honesty, spontaneity and charisma. What a winning combination.

Advertisers know that dogs are good at conveying messages. They reduce tension between the seller and the buyer. They are affable, avuncular and friendly spokespersons and help viewers retain the sales pitch. People respond to them for a variety of reasons.

First of all, dogs hold people's attention. When an international manufacturer of detergents tested seven-day recall of a variety of ads for their product, they found that if they associated their product with someone playing a typical housewife, thirty-two per cent of viewers remembered the product a week later. If the product was associated with a bird, thirty-eight per cent remembered. If a famous personality was used, forty-eight per cent remembered and if a horse was used, the figure rose to sixty-two per cent. But when a dog was used, seventy-seven per cent remembered the product. Dogs are excellent at attracting and holding people's attention.

Advertisers also use dogs for anthropomorphic reasons, to imply fidelity, sympathy and faithfulness. Symbolically, dogs are like Peter Pan; they never grow old. Advertisers use robust, healthy dogs to associate spontaneity, youth, vigour and health with their products. Refined and attractive breeds are associated with some products because people appreciate good design and associate the looks of the dog with the advertised product. In other circumstances, advertisers use dogs because they signify masculine values: strength, speed, companionship and outdoor activities. When advertisers want to associate their products with nature they prefer to use mongrels, 'natural' dogs.

In an affluent world advertisers use dogs for products directed at specific sectors of the market. A dog in an ad means two-and-a-half kids, the suburbs and a Volvo. Advertisers use dogs as a metaphor, to symbolize what cannot be shown explicitly. Labrador pups sell toilet paper – the pup is soft and gentle so the product must be too. Advertisers, more than many social scientists, understand intuitively that dogs are totems of the human past. The social scientist Lionel Tiger was eloquent about how people respond to dogs when he said, 'In a denatured society in which contact with the flow of natural process requires a conscious choice, the existence of domestic animals offers the opportunity to affirm – let me put it boldly but not sentimentally – the value, charm and fierce significance of life itself'. Advertisers understand this perfectly.

53. *Why are there such differences in families? How can I tell which family is right for me?*

Each family is a unique entity but there are statistical guidelines that suggest what type of family is best for particular dogs.

Let's start with their homes. People who live in bungalows and detached homes like dogs the most, followed by people who live in semi-detached or terraced houses. People in flats like dogs the least, the higher the apartment building the less they like dogs. Home owners like dogs more than people who rent their homes, and people with gardens like dogs more than people without gardens.

Next, check out where people live. Those in the open countryside like dogs most. As the concentration of people increases, love of dogs decreases. There are small but consistent drops of five per cent in dog liking in village folk, then town folk and finally among city folk.

The size of the family unit and the age of the children are other good indicators of what type of family is best for dogs. The most dog-loving families are small units of two or three people. The least dog friendly is the single person living alone. Dog popularity decreases as the size of the family increases but once numbers reach five, popularity remains constant. Dogs are best loved in families where the children are between six and fifteen years old.

Dogs are more likely to find homes in some countries than in others, but this does not necessarily infer different degrees of liking dogs. Within countries, liking dogs is also a regional phenomenon. For example, in Britain, dogs are loved most in the Northeast, Midlands and Southwest and liked least in London.

Finally, the most important factor influencing which home is best for a dog is whether that home already has livestock. Needless to say, dog owners are most likely to enjoy another dog in their home while cat owners are least likely, with caged bird owners perched on the fence, as it were, between these two groups.

54. *Why have they left me with the kids. Isn't that irresponsible?*

Yes, it is irresponsible. This is a phenomenon related to education. The more advanced the education of the parents the less likely it is that a dog will be left with the children.

People say they get dogs for the children. Many understand that, while caring for a dog is an excellent learning experience, it remains the parents' responsibility to care for the canine. This is a healthy attitude. It means that parents understand that a dog is not simply a toy; that it is not an item to be discarded. Sensible parents never leave children unattended with dogs. They never agree to look after a neighbour's dog then give the dog to the children to exercise. They understand that dogs have their own individual needs but also that dogs are potentially dangerous. They do not put their children at risk.

This behaviour pattern requires some thought on the part of people and is more likely to occur among those with either a university education or an inherent desire to learn and to understand, a desire that has led to that person reading and learning in the absence of the availability of higher education. Irresponsibility will always be a facet of the behaviour of certain people. These individuals remain irresponsible regardless of education. For many others, the road to increased responsibility for dogs remains in people understanding the dog's specific needs.

55. *I'm planning on emigrating. What is the best country to live in?*

It depends what a dog is interested in. Some countries, for example the Scandinavian countries, have advanced dog protection laws. In others, like Switzerland, dogs are so well protected that it is illegal to leave them outdoors overnight. Great Britain has excellent humane welfare laws, almost as good as the Nordic countries, but also the most poorly worded and potentially dangerous national dog control legislation in Europe or North America.

Many countries have legislation to control dangerous dogs. British legislation imputes guilt (and demands incarceration) until innocence is proved. It was directed at American Pit Bull Terriers and a few other breeds but has been successfully used to order the destruction of dogs with, for example, Labrador and Great Dane parents – not because the progeny caused any harm, or were even accused of causing harm, but because their cross breeding resulted in their looking like American Pit Bull Terriers. While this legislation remains unaltered Britain remains a dangerous country for dogs of a certain look to live in.

Dog ownership varies considerably from country to country. If a dog enjoys meeting other dogs, the country with the highest dog population might be best. Here is a list of countries with the percentages of dog owning homes in each one:

Australia	38%
United States	38%
France	34%
Ireland	34%
Canada	32%
Belgium	30%

Czech Republic . . .	30%
Hungary	30%
Luxembourg	30%
Denmark	28%
United Kingdom . . .	26%
Spain	25%
Italy	23%
Slovenia	23%
Portugal	20%
The Netherlands . . .	19%
Norway	18%
Sweden	18%
Austria	15%
Germany	13%
Japan	12%
Greece	10%
Switzerland	10%

These figures give good clues about where it is best to live. If a dog has a choice it should choose an English-speaking country. More homes are available in these regions than elsewhere. Failing that, dogs should choose French-speaking countries where only slightly fewer households are on offer. These figures suggest that dogs are unwise to choose German-speaking countries, or other countries in which Germanic languages are spoken. In that sense, these figures are misleading. While there are fewer homes available for dogs in these regions, the quality of home care may well be superior. For example, in French-speaking countries only one-and-a-half per cent of the dog's food budget is spent on dog snacks, while in Germany dog owners spend fifteen per cent of the dog's food budget on snack foods.

CHAPTER FOUR

The Hidden Health of Dog Owners and Dogs

DOGJOG 2000 — FULLY DOGMATIC

56. *It's absurd; I'm not a drug, how can I possibly lower someone's blood pressure?*

It is a scientific fact. People with dogs have lower blood pressure and if they have heart attacks they are more likely to be alive a year later than people who don't own dogs. That ability to survive is not related to the severity of the heart attack, age, sex, financial worth or psychological profile, although it is related to the person's social support. It is not related to personality type. Extensive studies in England show that so-called 'Type A' personalities, with high-risk lifestyles, are just as common among dog owners as among cat owners or people who do not own pets. In fact, in the largest study, in Coventry, 'Type A' personalities were more likely to own pets.

There is more. Independent scientists questioned the first published reports in the 1980s that connected pet ownership to an increased likelihood of being alive a year after having a heart attack. In the early 1990s, sceptical Australian cardiologists conducted a major survey of over 5,500 people attending a cardiovascular disease risk clinic in Melbourne, looking for any relationship between dogs and the risk of heart attacks.

At this clinic, patients completed a questionnaire on their eating, exercise and smoking habits. They were weighed and the amount of fat in their body mass calculated. They answered questions about their personal and family history of heart disease. Their blood pressure was measured and a blood sample was taken for plasma triglyceride and cholesterol measurements. All of these factors are known to be related to increased or decreased risk of cardiovascular disease. In this study, after these routines had been completed, the cardiologists added a final question about pet ownership.

When the results were analysed they revealed that male dog

owners had significantly lower plasma triglyceride and cholesterol levels than non-dog owners and also slightly, but significantly, lower systolic blood pressure. Women dog owners aged
between forty and forty-nine had significantly lower systolic
blood pressure than women who did not own dogs. They also
had lower plasma triglyceride levels (heart disease is the major
cause of death in this age group in women in Australia and
other countries). The same beneficial results were seen in cat
owners.

The results were unexpected because the scientists had set
out to show that dog ownership was *not* related to lowered risk
of heart disease. So, they went back and looked for other
reasons to explain the reduced risk of heart attacks in pet
owners.

There were no differences in body mass indexes between
pet owners and non-pet owners. Their smoking habits were
similar, but pet owners reported that they ate more takeaway
food and drank more alcohol than non-pet owners. Pet
owners also ate more meat. All of these are factors that increase the risk of cardiovascular disease, not decrease it. Both
groups had similar salt and egg consumption. Dog owners
did, however, take more exercise.

The social and financial backgrounds of these two groups
were similar, as was their level of education. All of these factors were similar to the Australian national average. (Non-pet
owners had marginally higher incomes and slightly more –
two per cent more – had completed tertiary or university
education.)

Cardiologists know that a one per cent drop in cholesterol
level is associated with a two-fold reduction in the risk of
death from cardiovascular disease. In this study the cholesterol level in pet owners was two per cent lower than in
non-pet owners. (The triglyceride level was thirteen per cent

lower in pet owners.) And while the difference in blood pressure was only slight, from the aspect of reducing the risk of heart attack it is substantial and surprisingly similar to another independent study in the United States.

In this study people were randomly selected from patients in a nationwide cardiac arrhythmia suppression trial. The researchers observed that dog owners were significantly less likely to die during the year following treatment than non-dog owners. The Americans calculated a three per cent reduction in the probability of death from a heart attack, surprisingly similar to the Australians' calculation of a four per cent reduction. In the United States alone this means 30,000 fewer deaths each year.

The cardiologists concluded, with some reluctance, that there is a relationship between pet ownership and reduced risk factors for heart disease, including reduced blood pressure. Of course, there is no evidence that a dog is the *cause* of this healthy finding. It is still a classic example of the chicken and the egg. Which came first, the dog leading to reduced cardiac disease risk factors, or a personality profile associated with reduced cardiac disease risk factors but also with a tendency to keep pets? Who knows.

57. *It has also been written that simply by living with me people have less backache and fewer colds. Is that true?*

Now this seems to be absolutely true among dog-owning populations in Europe, Australia and North America. Pet owners might not know it but secretly they have fewer minor health problems and better psychological wellbeing than people without pets. Dog owners are healthier than cat owners.

The first good examination of this phenomenon was carried out at Cambridge University in England, the most recent at the University of California. Using an accepted analytical method called 'self analysis', social scientists asked people about their general health before they acquired a dog, immediately after acquiring the dog and then throughout the following year. They asked the same questions of cat owners.

The Cambridge survey asked people to complete a 'General Health Questionnaire', a well used and approved survey method that measures the incidence of minor health problems. The list included:

Headaches
Hay fever
Sleeping difficulties
Constipation
Eye trouble
Bad back
Nerves
Colds and flu
General tiredness
Kidney and bladder trouble

Painful joints
Trouble with the feet
Difficulty concentrating
Palpitations and breathlessness
Trouble with the ears
Worrying over every little thing
Indigestion and stomach trouble
Sinus trouble and catarrh
Persistent cough
Faints and dizziness

Doctors call these *minor* health complaints. No wonder so many don't take their patients' worries seriously.

The people who conduct these surveys know that there is always a seasonal incidence of minor health problems and, using statistical methods, it is possible to eliminate these blips. When they looked at the results they saw that people reported a significant reduction in minor health problems a month after acquiring a kitten or pup. At six months, this improvement was no longer evident in cat owners and the incidence of minor health problems had reverted to its previous level. But in dog owners the improvement was constant, still there a year after acquiring the pup, when the survey concluded. Using the statistics from the survey, if the incidence of minor health problems was '4' before the survey began, among dog owners it dropped to '2' and remained there.

The Californian scientists repeated this study and got the same results. But they added one more group, people acquiring new dogs who already had dogs. In these circumstances there was no change in the baseline of self-reported minor health problems. They concluded that if you already have a dog you cannot improve your health further by getting another dog.

At the same time the English and American workers were analysing their results, a 6,000-household survey was being carried out in Australia. One of the curiosities of that survey was that dog owners attended their doctor eight per cent less often than non-dog owners.

If you ask me, I think it is the change in a person's lifestyle after getting a dog that reduces minor health problems, not the dog per se. Sure, there is the sound evidence that stroking a dog reduces the owner's blood pressure (just as stroking reduces the dog's blood pressure). And there is sound evidence of reduced cardiac risk among dog owners. But as far as minor health problems are concerned, I think the obvious reason why dog owners are healthier is because they get more exercise. After all, that is the major difference between cat and dog owners. Cat owners reported better health after getting their cats but this could be attributed to the novelty value of a new kitten, a value that disappears within a few months. A dog owner's health seems to improve permanently after getting a new dog, but not if that person is already a dog owner and getting the exercise anyway.

Professor James Serpell, who published his Cambridge study in the Royal Society of Medicine Journal, says that walking cannot, on its own, account for all of the reported health benefits. But that is the difference, the *only* difference, between cat owners and dog owners. Go figure.

58. *So, are dog owners healthier than people who don't own dogs?*

Possibly, although the evidence is only now beginning to accumulate. People certainly *think* that dog owners are healthier. In a 10,000-household survey in Britain, seventy-four per cent of people believed that dogs improve their owner's health and seventy-three per cent felt that dogs help owners relax, and that relaxing is good for people's health.

It looks like dogs somehow increase resistance to heart disease and, either directly or indirectly, enhance good health by reducing the incidence of minor health problems. But, don't forget, dog owners also have an increased risk of being injured accidentally by their dogs or of picking up transmissible diseases like ringworm or scabies from them. The dog owners' best-kept secret is not telling anyone how often they are bitten by their dogs. In Britain over a quarter of a million dog bites are registered yearly, but those are only bites reported to hospitals or the police.

These dog-bite figures are somewhat surprising because they show that the popular, large guarding breeds like German Shepherds, Dobermans and Rottweilers are no more likely to bite than average, while the seemingly more companionable West Highland White and Yorkshire Terriers, Chihuahuas and Toy Poodles are the real menaces. People are more willing to put up with attacks from these small dogs without visiting a hospital for treatment than people who are attacked by large dogs. No one knows the exact incidence of these minor bites or how deleterious they are to human health.

One interesting aspect of dogs possibly being good for people's health – or of contributing to better health – emerges from a completely unrelated finding in the field of hospital design. At a Swedish hospital, architects asked doctors to monitor the post-surgical period in patients admitted to that hospital for an operation on their gall bladders. Some patients spent their post-surgical period in rooms overlooking open countryside. Others spent the period in rooms overlooking external walls of the hospital.

As in any progressive hospital, pain relief was on patient demand. The doctors noted that patients who looked out of their windows on to open countryside asked for less pain relief medication than patients who looked out on to brick walls. Those in rooms overlooking the countryside were discharged from hospital, on average, one-and-a-half days earlier than those in rooms with windows facing walls.

This study, published in an architectural journal, could be evidence to indicate that when people are exposed to the outside world – to nature – they feel better and heal faster. This should not be surprising, as people do go out into the countryside alone to feel 'healed'. Nature has a healing effect on the mind. It turns people's thoughts outwards, away from themselves. If that is true of all nature then the dog, simply by being what it is – an uncomplicated, sociably gregarious product of the natural world – is good for people's health.

59. *Big question: do dog owners live longer than other people?*

There is no evidence to suggest that they do. If dogs secretly affect the health of people, it is through the quality of life and a feeling of wellbeing. There is no evidence, certainly not yet, that quantity is affected. (If there were evidence, life insurance companies would find it before anyone else, and offer reduced premiums for dogs owners, as many property insurance companies already do for dog-owning property owners.) Let me give some examples of how quality rather than quantity is affected.

If people develop Alzheimer's disease, dogs make a difference to their lives. In Nebraska, in the United States, when scientists monitored people who spent time with a dog visiting a nursing home, these people smiled more, leaned forward and touched more, used words of praise and showed more physical warmth than they did in the absence of the dog. In another study in Queensland, Australia, elderly residents in nursing homes showed less confusion, depression, fatigue and tension, and showed more vigour after resident dogs were introduced. In a Canadian study in Ontario, elderly dog owners were more likely to be able to perform routine daily activities than non-pet owners. These improvements remained as long as the dogs lived in the nursing homes.

Similar beneficial changes have been reported so many times from so many countries, involving so many different groups of people in such a variety of institutions that it is no longer news. Large multidisciplinary international scientific meetings are held every few years for people to share their knowledge and information on how dogs improve the quality of life.

A common theme emerges from these scientific meetings. The financial wizard Malcolm Forbes once said, 'Everybody has to be somebody to somebody to be anybody'. What Forbes explained, with pithy succinctness, researchers discover in search of a Ph.D. People have important needs like security and exercise and slightly less important needs like possessions and sexual activity. Their most important needs are food and warmth but also companionship and being *needed*. Dogs are good for people's health because dogs need people. Dogs innately know that the best way to have a friend is to be one. Fortunately for them they have facial muscles that allow them to express a wide range of human-looking emotions, including dependency. Dog owners do not live longer, but the constancy of dogs, the always changing but never changing aspect of living Peter-Pan lives, caught between nature and culture in a state of perpetual innocence and dependence, acts as a rock in some people's lives. Life does not last longer but it is filled with more contentment.

60. *If I'm so good for them, why don't they all let me sleep on their beds?*

Hygiene. People can be fastidious creatures. What is perfectly acceptable for a dog – a tangy coat or a few fellow travellers wandering around in the undergrowth – is anathema to most dog owners.

A dog's chances of being allowed to sleep on the bed are directly related to its size. On average, certainly in the United States and Britain, dogs have a fifty-nine per cent chance of being allowed up on people's beds. That percentage increases for small dogs but decreases quite dramatically for large dogs, although even breeds the size of Golden Retrievers still have over a thirty per cent chance of hopping up on the bed and not being reprimanded. Big, innocent brown eyes help a lot.

Today, most dog owners are aware that there are health benefits from letting a dog share in family life. That does not mean that the dog should be converted into a health god to whom sacrifices are made, such as the freedom to sleep where it wishes. Sensible people understand that a dog can enhance family wellbeing but still be treated like a dog, which means sleeping in its own bed if the owner so wishes.

61. *Why do some other people think I am medically or physically dangerous to them?*

Because dogs *are* medically or physically dangerous to some people. Dogaholics, dog obsessives, dog worshippers – they all get carried away with the values of dogs and forget dogs are modified wolves with all the dangers associated with modified wolves.

Medically, the most lethal danger is from rabies, a fatal disease which can be transmitted by a dog's bite and which creates an almost paranoid fear in many people, especially people in countries where the disease does not exist. Britain, Ireland, Japan, Australia, New Zealand, Hawaii and other 'isolated' places do not have rabies in their wildlife and have quarantine laws to prevent the disease from arriving. Europeans are fortunate, in a peculiar way, because the strain of rabies present in Europe lives primarily in foxes. In other regions, India for example, the dog is the primary carrier of this disease. In Europe there wasn't a human death from rabies transmitted by a European dog for seventy years, until a Romanian child died from a rabid dog bite in 1996.

Scientists have known for over a decade that quarantine is not the only secure method of preventing rabies from entering a region. An anti-rabies vaccination with a follow-up check that a dog has produced genuine protection from the disease is equally effective. In the early 1990s both Norway and Sweden – hygienically speaking squeaky-clean countries with a large reservoir of wildlife to protect – dropped dog and cat quarantine as their primary means of rabies control and replaced it with a vaccination and identification programme. Both scientists and the public in these enlightened countries abandoned their paranoia about dogs bringing in rabies from abroad. This is not the case elsewhere. The public in other countries secretly and publicly feel that allowing even vaccinated dogs into their rabies-free regions is an unacceptable risk. So much for paranoia.

Worries about physical dangers from dogs are better founded. Dogs bite and they bite surprisingly frequently. Different breeds bite in different ways; terriers bite, shake and relax, Bull Terriers and their relatives bite, shake and hold on, Labradors bite and release. When dogs attack livestock, different breeds go for different parts of the body; Bull Terriers bite lips and shoulders, Rottweilers bite the neck and muzzle, German Shepherds bite the flanks and Kelpies, Australian descendants of 'heelers', bite the hind quarters. When people are bitten, the size of the victim determines where they are bitten; children are bitten on the face and arms, adults on the legs and rump.

The most common reason people give for being afraid of dogs is that a dog bit them in childhood. (Cultural differences are equally important.) Doctors estimate that up to ten per cent of children are bitten by dogs during their formative years. This is an exceedingly high number. The fact that far fewer than ten per cent of the population actively dislike dogs is a good indication of how powerful the human attraction is to the species, even when dogs bite so frequently.

62. *I've got a very personal question: do people seriously have sex with my kind?*

Yes, but it is so uncommon that when incidents emerge they are front-page news in newspapers and the subject of doctoral theses in the social sciences.

Bestiality, sex with animals, is a social taboo in most human cultures. People do get obvious enjoyment from petting and stroking their dogs and, at one time, some writers thought that this was a form of human sexual gratification, that petting a dog was a sexual turn-on. They failed to understand that it was comforting and soothing rather than sexually arousing, that it was a return to the intimacy of childhood, not an alternative to the intimacy of adult sexual encounters.

It is also true that some dog owners allow their dogs to masturbate on their arms and legs but they do so either because they do not know how to stop the dog from masturbating, or because they feel this is acceptable behaviour for a dog to carry out, in the absence of dogs of the other sex, in the privacy of its own home and with a consenting adult. The pleasure the owner gets is not sexual but rather that of allowing a dog to do what the owner thinks a dog has got to do.

Some owners may take their obligation to provide all aspects of a normal canine existence one step further and actively masturbate their dogs, but this is probably uncommon.

Sex with any animal is rare but with dogs probably even more so because of the size of a typical dog. There was one widely reported incident of child abuse in Sweden involving a father, his young daughter and a dog, but this form of behaviour is only a manifestation of a perverted extreme. Biological imperatives have been refined for millions of years and, overwhelmingly, people are attracted to have sex with other people. Sometimes the wires get crossed and people are attracted to have sex with their own sex, biologically pretty much dead-end behaviour. If a person is sexually attracted to dogs, it is quite certain that the person will hide their inclinations, because society finds such behaviour grossly unacceptable. It is safe to say that the overwhelmingly vast majority of dogs may feel safe from this form of human predation.

63. *I like to leave scent markers to tell other dogs I have visited. After all, people have visiting cards and these are mine. Why won't they let me dump where I want to?*

Many people fail to understand that urine and faeces are not simply waste products; they are a dog's aroma-filled personal items, intentionally left in a variety of places to act as informative 'newspapers' for other dogs. People do not treat their own body waste in a similar fashion, preferring to dump it all in designated latrine sites. Fortunately for people, dogs – females in particular – are willing to copy this human behaviour. Male dogs take more intensive coaxing.

64. *How can I trust a vet who smiles at me then stabs me in the back?*

Veterinarians are simply people with, hopefully, a little more knowledge and understanding of the physical and emotional needs of dogs than other people. They gain this knowledge by studying about dogs, then by observing them. In the long term, observation and experience are of more importance that theoretical knowledge.

When dogs first meet vets they do not fear them any more than they do other people. But then curious things happen. The vet picks up the dog and puts it on a table. Any sensible dog understands that this is an overt act of dominance on the vet's part; the dog is on a slippery surface and knows if it jumps down it might hurt itself.

The vet continues to behave in a dominant fashion although the vet might not even realize what he or she is doing. Unblinkingly, the vet looks straight into the dog's eyes. If the dog tries to turn away the vet returns the dog's head to a full frontal position. This is powerful intimidation. Then the vet examines the dog's body. He looks in the ears, at the lips and raises the tail – all actions of a dominant dog. He might even insert something cold and hard into the dog's rectum, an overwhelming act of intimidation.

By now any sensitive dog might feel threatened, but there is more. Just as a dominant dog attacks the scruff of another dog's neck, the vet grabs a handful of skin. And in a grotesque parody of a bite, instead of sinking his teeth in, he inserts an artificial tooth – a sharp metal object, through which he shoots irritating fluid. All the time the vet continues to whisper sweet nothings into the dog's ears. No wonder a dog feels mixed up and threatened the next time it visits a veterinary clinic.

With a little thought and tact vets can make visits to a veterinary clinic less fraught for a dog. They can avoid direct eye contact when dogs first arrive and allow them to sniff around to pick up a few messages. They can offer tasty food snacks when circumstances permit, or toys if they seem appropriate. They can examine dogs on the floor or on laps or on their owner's knees, where dogs feel less intimidated, rather than on high tables. And they can provide distractions: sights, sounds, smells and tastes when they have to do painful or intimidating things like take a temperature or give an injection. When a vet is considerate and understanding, a dog will trust him – even when it is stabbed in the back.

65. *If they really love me so much why do they constantly envelop me in a toxic cloud of nerve gas?*

People hate fleas. It's pathological. They hate them so much they will go to dangerous extremes to keep them out of their homes. Curiously, although people will take great care to feed their dogs nutritious food, to prevent contagious disease by vaccinating their dogs and to prevent accidents by obedience training, unwittingly, they are willing to cover dogs in poisonous nerve gas. Some even make their dogs swallow it. (They do it to sheep too, dipping them in it. And while people, including doctors and government officials, recognize that farmers who use nerve gas – organophosphates – on livestock are themselves at risk, so far there's not been much thought for the sheep.)

Using nerve gas is unnecessary because there are gentler methods to prevent fleas from taking up residence on dogs (and people), and gentler methods of eliminating them once they have arrived.

Prevention, as always, is easier, cheaper and safer than cure. And the best way to prevent fleas is to use a biological product on both dogs and their environment that prevents fleas from reproducing. Biological products do not contaminate the dog with dangerous chemicals, they only affect the fleas' ability to reproduce. These flea-control methods can be used in the dog's environment, on carpets and the dog's bedding. Certain sprays prevent existing flea eggs from hatching, while other products can be given as pills. They don't kill fleas but when a flea has a meal on the dog, effectively it swallows flea birth control. It can't reproduce and it dies off. Because most dogs don't mind the odd flea bite, this is a very effective way to get rid of these pests.

For dogs that are sensitive to fleas, other safer, non-nerve gas products are available as sprays or shampoos. Any flea that hops on to a treated dog commits suicide. People are edgy about fleas because of a little historical baggage – after all it was the rat flea that spread bubonic plague throughout Europe. While dog fleas can be irritating to people and even cause allergic reactions in some, there is scant evidence that they transmit serious diseases to people.

66. *First they wouldn't let me fool around with other dogs, then they sterilized me. Who gave them the right?*

They did. People assume they have the right to make all decisions about all aspects of animal life. Many think it is a divine right, a God-given right.

Dogs need to face reality. People are the dominant species on this planet, dominant in the sense that their behaviour is more influential than the behaviour of all other animals. It may be that the biomass of ants is greater than the biomass of humans but ants use very few other living things for their own selfish purposes. People have the capacity to denude forests, contaminate the greatest lakes and rivers in the world, breed and kill animals as they wish and to sterilize any dog they choose.

I am not saying that this is a bad bargain for dogs. In fact, it has been an incredibly good bargain. In giving up the right to independence and the right to choose its own mates, the dog has become the most successful of all members of the canine family. Over two hundred million dogs live worldwide. No other canine species – wolves, coyotes, foxes or others – has been even remotely as successful at being fruitful and multiplying.

The dog and the human are parasites on each other but are what scientists call saprophytic parasites; they benefit each other. For the rewards of security, food, comfort and good health, dogs have given up the right to procreate according to their own selection processes. People make the choice for people reasons, not dog reasons. There is no evidence that people, other than a minority fringe who believe that all animals should breed according to their own perceptions of the survival of the fittest, rather than by human perceptions (and who also believe that all animals, including dogs, should live independently of human control), will give up this control at any time in the future.

67. *People get vaccinated against diseases when they are children, then that's it. Why do I get vaccinated so often, is this a secret medical scam?*

I do not think so but I cannot be completely certain.

People can be vaccinated during childhood against a variety of diseases, such as polio, chicken pox, whooping cough and measles, and develop lifelong protection. In other instances, for example yellow fever, typhoid fever, cholera, hepatitis and rabies, people need to boost their protection with repeat injections at varying intervals.

Childhood protection offers successful lifelong immunity against some human diseases and, remember, humans live more than five times longer than dogs. It seems logical then that puppyhood protection should offer lifelong protection against at least some dog diseases. Maybe it does.

It is possible that effective early vaccination against distemper does offer lifelong protection, as long as the vaccine is effective in the first place. When distemper virus crossed the border from Russia into Finland in the mid 1990s, Finnish dogs that had been vaccinated against distemper contracted the disease. The vaccine offered no protection against the Russian strain of the virus.

Vaccines against other canine diseases, hepatitis for example, might provide similar long-term protection, but vaccines against other diseases such as parvovirus are only effective for a relatively short period of time – nine to eighteen months. Arbitrarily, vets revaccinate yearly against these diseases, often including vaccine against diseases like distemper, 'to be on the safe side'.

It is at least theoretically possible that by doing so vets are not erring 'on the safe side' but rather contributing to other problems. As veterinary medicine has become more sophisticated, the diagnosis of disorders of the immune system has increased. No one knows whether there is a real increased incidence or whether vets are just better at making this difficult diagnosis. If there is a genuine increase in 'immune incompetence' diseases, some feel this may be related to the frequent provocation of the immune system caused by the injection of 'multivalent' vaccines; vaccines that protect against many diseases through one small injection.

This is only a theoretical, not a proven or even widely held belief. It is a niggle, but one that is potentially more important than the possibility of excessive vaccinations being given for the financial reward of pharmaceutical companies and vets.

68. *I walk slowly and I have trouble getting up. I'm owned by decent people, why can't they see I'm in pain and do something about it?*

People cry when they are hurt. People complain when they are uncomfortable. And they think that because these are their reactions to pain, dogs behave the same way when they are hurt.

Of course, dogs are far more stoic than people. Dogs suffer silently, unless a pain is sudden and acute – like when someone steps on a dog's foot. Many people fail to read the dog's body language of chronic pain. Depending upon where the pain is, a dog will carry its head in a more concentrated way, its tail will beat in a more rhythmic fashion, it might lean forward or arch its back or favour a painful leg by limping. It might no longer spring up from a resting position but rather get up front first then drag up its hind quarters, or it might find it difficult to lie down and will crash instead of finding an intentional position. Dogs with chronic pain in the hind quarters no longer fly upstairs, while dogs with chronic forequarter pain are apprehensive about going downstairs. Dogs with chronic pain slow down earlier during their exercise than they used to, or should do, for their age.

When dogs suffer from chronic pain they approach their affliction the way doctors tell people to contend with their chronic pain; dogs get on with life, they live with their pain. They don't spend their time thinking of the way they used to be. Just as people should do but find almost impossible to do, a dog takes as its point of reference its period of worst pain and still enjoys food, affection and play. It does not get morose.

Because dogs do not complain, even decent, knowledgeable, caring and considerate owners often fail to understand that changes in the dog's rhythm of life have been caused by pain. They often feel that their dog is 'slowing down' because it is 'growing older'. The most observant dog owners see changes in body language and understand that these are associated with pain but even some of these people feel that pain is a regrettable yet unavoidable part of ageing.

Sometimes a degree of pain is unavoidable but in the vast majority of instances a dog's chronic pain can be easily diminished, especially pains associated with ageing. People forget that there have been great advances in pain control for humans and that these advances apply to dogs too. When circumstances permit, tried and trusted aspirin remains a powerful, safe and inexpensive method of pain control. But when there are medical reasons for avoiding aspirin, other newer and more potent painkilling medicines are available.

There are various alternative ways of reducing the discomfort of chronic pain for dogs – deep heat, ultrasound, acupuncture, massage, even skin patches of slow-release painkillers. The intensity of pain can almost always be diminished but this depends completely upon a dog's owner realizing that his or her uncomplaining dog is in pain in the first place.

69. *I hear I'm a health hazard to people but what about the other side of the picture. Are people a health hazard to me?*

Critically so. After all, people drive cars and cars kill more dogs than any natural predators. People use weapons and shoot dogs either by intention or by accident. People neglect dogs but hide that fact from other people. But, most importantly, people are lethal to all dogs because they have the right to make life and death decisions, to decide whether a dog survives or dies.

The most critical time in a dog's life is its first year. More dogs die during this year because their owners choose to have them destroyed than at any other time in a dog's life, including the advanced years. People usually make this lethal decision because of the dog's behaviour – often perfectly normal behaviour that people find unpleasant or unexpected.

Dogs are destroyed because they are no longer puppies. Stupid people forget that cuddly balls of fluff grow up. Dogs are destroyed because they urinate or defecate in the house. Idiotic people blame their dogs. They are too dim to understand that this is not a dog's fault but wholly theirs. Dogs are easily trained to use latrine sites. Dogs are destroyed because they have a zest for life. Foolish people expect young dogs to act like geriatrics, to sit around all day maintaining muscle tone through isometric exercises rather than from real workouts. Dogs are destroyed because people change their minds. Selfish, self-centred people do not have the mental capacity to understand that a dog is real; it is sentient, it thinks and feels.

Even after one year of age, people pass death sentences on dogs because it is so easy to do. People's personal relationships change and dogs die. People move and dogs die. No dog has a say in the matter if circumstances have left it in the hands of unthinking, uncaring people.

A final critical period is reached when a dog becomes elderly. But if a dog does attain an advanced age the health hazard of an unnecessary death sentence changes. It is no longer the result of people's selfish behaviour, now it can be caused by love. People ask for death sentences to be passed on their dogs because they feel it is 'the humane thing to do'. This is not necessarily so.

With advancing years, dogs develop behavioural and mental changes similar to Alzheimer's disease in people. In one study of dogs with an average age of thirteen and a half, almost fifty per cent of them exhibited at least eleven manifestations of deteriorating mental functions, including activity, attention, awareness, hearing and house-training. Curiously, people were more concerned about their dogs sleeping more or showing reduced activity and attention than about disturbances in house-training. It seems that people are more tolerant of toileting problems in ageing dogs than they are of similar problems in ageing humans, a common 'last straw' that leads to the nursing home for many elderly people.

Dogs are often killed when these senile changes occur because people feel that their dogs are suffering. They forget that just like people with Alzheimer's, friends and relatives suffer more than the patient. They remember how that person once was and are pained to see such a ravaging deterioration. But in advanced senility the patient cannot remember how things once were. So it is with dogs. People remain a potentially lethal health hazard to dogs as long as they respond to their dog's behaviour in an unthinking manner.

70. *I'm always itchy. I can't sleep without jumping up and scratching. Can I possibly be allergic to my owners?*

Absolutely. People seldom realize it but they are often the hidden cause of their dog's itchy skin condition. The problem concerns the way people live.

In this century, people have created warmer, softer home environments than ever before. Central heating is normal in most countries with a temperate climate. Wall-to-wall carpeting is common in countries such as Great Britain, Canada and the United States. These two facts have lead to an explosion in the population of house dust mites and these are a common cause of allergic skin reaction in some dogs, especially in certain breeds like West Highland White Terriers, Bull Terriers and English Setters. But there is more.

There was a time when a well-loved dog slept in the kitchen, or in a kennel. Not now. People are more intimate with dogs. Most permit, even demand, that their dogs have access to their bedrooms. But this exposes allergic dogs to yet another cause of itchy coats and watery eyes: sloughing human skin – people dander. The two most common indoor allergens that provoke an allergic response in dogs are human dander and dust mites that live off human dander (or, to be more accurate, the dust mites' droppings).

The only way dogs can avoid these potential irritants is to change their owners' lifestyles. Wall-to-wall carpets, especially in bedrooms, should be abolished and replaced by hard floors. Rugs should be small enough to be cleaned easily. People should allow more fresh air in their homes, opening windows to drive out some of the suspension of house dust mite droppings that always hangs in the air. Sensible dogs should never sleep on their owners' beds. These are disgusting places. After only a few years virtually one-third of the weight of a person's pillow consists of human dander; dead dust mites and their droppings. It's the same with people's mattresses. Although people are quick to recognize that they can be allergic to dogs, it is just as likely that dogs are allergic to people.

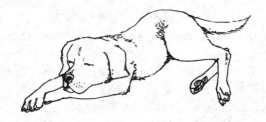

71. *Give me the choice and I'd prefer a haunch of venison. But what do they feed me? Dehydrated astronaut food. Crunchy bits in pretty shapes. Why?*

This is odd. Only a few human generations ago dogs were fed scraps, offal and waste. Country dogs lived off fly-blown sheep carcasses and city dogs lived off the leftovers from people's plates.

Then manufacturers invented 'dog food'. The first dog food was simply hardtack seamen's biscuits that had got too maggot-infested even for sailors. Though the biscuit was rather tasteless, manufacturers realized there was a market for dog food. They continued to sell hard dog biscuit but also invented tinned foods, made from meat unfit for human consumption.

By the middle of this century both the sources for dog food and their manufacturing processes had changed. Reputable manufacturers no longer used products unfit for human consumption. Instead, they became efficient 'scavengers' searching for cheap surpluses of food produced for the human food chain. Europe, with its farm subsidies that favoured over-production, and North America, Australia and New Zealand, with their intensive agricultural industries that produced cheap protein, were constant sources of good quality protein. Most of this went into tinned food. To dogs, and their owners, it looked like processed meat and smelled like processed meat. Then something strange happened; manufacturers discovered that lots of people like to feed their dogs dry food out of boxes rather than wet food out of tins.

This cultural change began in the United States but rapidly spread to Canada and then Europe and beyond. Some of these dehydrated meat foods carried instructions to mix them with tepid water to make a gravy. Others were eaten straight from the box, like biscuits and cookies. No one knows why people's attitudes changed but within a decade, dehydrated, or dry, dog foods became overwhelming market leaders in North America and major market players in Europe.

Now, dog food manufacturers upped the ante. When they saw there was a sophisticated market demand for high-quality dog food, some started competing with manufacturers who processed foods for human consumption. Personally, I do not like this change because there is, and there will continue to be, a surplus of protein available for dog food. Manufacturers simply have to search and find it. By competing with people-food manufacturers they only drive up the price of processed people-food.

Dogs might like to chew on venison haunches or cow's knees but that does not provide a balanced diet. Premium dry foods from good manufacturers certainly do. The world's largest dog food manufacturers make certain that all the nutrients a dog needs are in these foods. And although they do not look particularly appetizing to people, they seem to be superbly tasty to most canines.

As for shape, different producers offer different shapes. These add texture to food – something important to dogs – but shape can also be symbolic. The most sophisticated Japanese complete dog food comes in the form of hearts. Not only does this add texture and improve biteability, it also permits owners to say something symbolic to their dogs as they pour their hearts into the food bowl.

72. *Rather than take food out of their own food chain, why don't people feed me the real thing, wild meat?*

They do not do so because of misguided political correctness. In many parts of the world, populations of wild animals are 'culled' – another way of saying killed – because of overgrazing or overpopulation leading to increased parasitic problems and other diseases. Seals are culled in Europe. Elephants are culled in South Africa. Deer are culled in North America and, most numerous of all, kangaroos are culled in Australia.

All these animals offer superb nutrients for dogs but animal lovers hate the idea of turning these excellent carcasses into dog food. Instead, they are burned or buried. It's a psychological thing. There is no logic involved.

73. *I hear terrible tales about other dogs being abused. What is the risk of my being battered? If I am, will anyone know? Will anyone help?*

Dogs, because they are dogs, are always at risk of being abused. Few people outside the dog's human family know. But if any people know that abuse is taking place there are organizations that will help, including the courts.

People have a most irrational attitude towards dogs. Dogs are *owned* by people and because dogs are possessions, they are sold, traded or discarded. Legislation exists to prevent cruelty to animals, but this usually applies only to extreme cruelty and seldom to benign neglect or the occasional kick

On the other hand, dogs are 'members of the family'. People develop an emotional attachment to dogs. People understand that dogs have feelings and emotions, that they can be distressed, anxious, agitated, happy, joyful or euphoric.

This dichotomy of human attitude – that a dog is a sentient being but also simply a possession – creates problems. A dog can be loved one minute and abused the next. It is treated as a member of the family, fed and cared for, then discarded when the family moves or simply tires of it.

Physical abuse comes easily. Dogs are trained to be sub-servient to their human family. This is easy for dogs because, as pack animals, most like to be members of the pack, to follow instructions. Few dogs really desire to be paramount leaders. Genetically, dogs are primed to be admonished and not run away and some people simply take advantage of this guilelessness. In a classically cartoon sense, the boss dumps on the employee, the employee goes home and dumps on his son, the son kicks the dog. Everyone wants a scapegoat.

In families where wives and children are abused there is a heightened likelihood that dogs too are battered. Some animal welfare agencies, especially the largest, work in conjunction with social service agencies responsible for monitoring children at risk. Those responsible for child welfare and those responsible for pet welfare should share information with each other. By doing so risk to both children and dogs might be reduced.

CHAPTER FIVE

The Hidden History of Dog Owners

74. *I was happy to be a wolf, I think. Why did people interfere in my ancestor's breeding in the first place?*

People did not actively decide to domesticate the wolf and create the dog. It was serendipity that led to the dog becoming the world's most successful carnivore (after people, of course).

The wolf made the first move. It decided it liked the new ecological niche that humans had created around their sites of permanent settlement, and moved in. This new 'man-made' environment had fewer dangers for wolves because people eliminated many of the dangers, such as other large predators. It offered good scavenging too, but there were drawbacks. Food could be scarce and, to people, wolf pups were cute and cuddly.

Survival in these conditions favoured smaller wolves with less fear of people, wolves willing to sneak or creep near the settlements to eat waste, or to trail human hunters and scavenge from their kills. With time, and it takes a surprisingly short time, several physical changes occurred in wolves. Without active human intervention in its breeding the wolf became smaller, its teeth became more crowded and its brain shrank. Enter the dog.

A smaller brain does not mean a dog is less intelligent than a wolf. A dog's brain is about thirty per cent smaller than a wolf's brain but the loss of size is restricted almost completely to the sensory part of the brain, the cerebellum. The thinking part, the cortex, did not shrink with domestication. In that sense the dog is no different from all other domesticated animals. When there is less need to hunt and forage, there is less need to rely upon sight, scent and hearing.

This process of 'self-domestication' was possible because

the wolf had, and still has, a very plastic and inventive mind. It was capable of altering its lifestyle to take advantage of changes in the environment that people created. (In England, foxes are doing this today by moving into towns and cities to scavenge from back gardens and discarded convenience foods like fried chicken and hamburgers. Russian studies show that in only seven generations foxes can become as tame as dogs, sitting on laps, coming when called and even barking like dogs.)

After the wolf made the first move, the second risk of living near humans, especially female humans, became significant. Orphaned or captured wolf pups were as attractive to people 15,000 years ago as they are today. Women in particular were willing to play with abandoned wolf pups, even breast feed them. People discovered that wolves were useful. If raised with humans they did not attack humans and could act as sentries. Equally, in time of hunger they offered ready meat. Accidental matings of captive wolves, raised with people, occurred but only the more amenable or useful offspring survived. The more aggressive pups were eaten. People did not actively interfere in the breeding process that created the dog. It created itself.

75. *When did people interfere in my breeding and, just out of curiosity, who were they?*

People probably began to select who would mate with whom about 12,000 years ago, probably somewhere in central Asia.

The first dogs to be born in human settlements bred among themselves without any human interference. Some of these camp-bred and raised wolf-dogs chose to accompany men when they left the settlement to hunt. Men noticed that some dogs were faster, or better at picking up an animal's scent trail, than others. These practical hunting companions were prized. Their value saved them from the stew pot and they lived long enough to mate and produce progeny that inherited their superior hunting ability. At some unknown time, some unknown person decided to let his hunting companion mate only with another excellent hunting dog. That was the true beginning of the dog's domestication by people.

Natural selection pressures created the dog out of the wolf but it was when people realized that by breeding one dog with attractive attributes to another with the same attributes that the dog's future became intertwined with that of people. Self-domestication began in the territory of the small Asian wolf, an animal that looks much like its dog relative the Australian Dingo. Active human intervention and the creation of distinctly enhanced characteristics such as speed or scent-following capacity probably took place where the earliest and most successful of all plant and animal domestications took place, China.

76. *Okay. So dogs guarded the camp and helped in the hunt. Why then did people make some of my relatives perfectly formed but useless little miniatures of me?*

It is true that early breeding emphasized practical uses for the dog such as a willingness to join men in the hunt and acting as sight- or scent-followers. Later, dogs were selectively bred for keenness to guard herds of sheep, goats and aurochs. In all of these circumstances dogs were practical, useful to man and good, large sources of meat when game was scarce.

People either controlled the dog's breeding or, when dogs bred randomly, saw the results of the mating. In natural circumstances, survival of the fittest favours those best adapted to the environment. In this new natural environment, survival of the fittest meant survival of those pups that appealed to people, either because they were practical or because they pricked human curiosity.

Bantamization, the production of perfectly formed small versions of the parents, occurs infrequently but it occurs naturally in virtually all species of plants and animals. Because of the original natural selection pressures on wolves favouring the survival of smaller individuals, a genetic predisposition to smallness is probably enhanced in dogs. In most ecological situations these bantams do not survive. Male dogs are bigger than female dogs because, just like humans, there is a tendency to fight for the right to mate. Scientists call this difference 'sexual dimorphism'. Males need to strut their stuff for females, to flex. A bantam dog is quite willing to behave this way but it has lost the advantage of size. It might ritually threaten another male for possession of a female in season, but get killed for its actions.

The dog's new ecological niche, living with people, now favoured the survival of curiosities like bantams because people were, and still are, an intensely inquisitive species. They are intrigued by the weird, the grotesque, the outlandish or strange. Bantams survived but may have needed extra help from people, help in the form of feeding and warmth. When people gave extra help they became more attached to these dogs simply because they had made more of an emotional investment in them. In return, the dogs were more attached to the people because of the increased handling they experienced when they were very young. These dogs survived the dinner pot because they offered less meat but also because they were people's companions. Miniaturization is not useless – on the contrary, it has been an extremely successful genetic shift. The dog's selfish genes are responsible for miniaturization. Dog breeders are simply the tools the dog's genes have used to ensure their survival.

77. *What about my brethren who are plodding arthritic dwarfs. Why did people let this happen?*

Initially, for the same reason they chose miniatures, or coat colour differences for that matter – curiosity. A malfunction of the pituitary gland occasionally occurs in all mammals, producing a dwarf. A dwarf pup is completely normal except its leg bones are dramatically shortened and it has enlarged joints. Few dwarf wolves ever reach maturity and virtually none are successful enough to reproduce. Human intervention changed that. The ancient Chinese, or their trading partners, actively bred accidental dwarf to accidental dwarf, producing a line of dogs that perpetuated this physical change. Dwarfed breeds of dogs existed in the royal dog kennels of China 5,000 years ago, a case of 'I've got something no one else has'.

Later on, perhaps 4,000 years ago, other breeders realized that these dwarfs might actually be useful. Breeders in ancient Persia discovered that dwarfed dogs, although no longer fleet footed, could be bred for enhanced scent following ability. The advantage of these dogs over dogs with long legs was that hunters could keep up with them more easily as they followed scent trails. Careful breeding initially took place in ancient Persia, an important centre of early breeding advances, but reached its most sophisticated level in mediaeval Europe. Swift, fleet footed dogs were introduced into Europe from Asia at least 3,000 years ago. They became the hunting companions of the nobility who hunted on horseback. By adding dwarf genes to these hunting hounds, a great variety of breeds now called Bassets, Laufhunds and Dachshunds became hunting companions of those who hunted on foot.

Although dwarfed, their legs were still reasonably well built, usually free from arthritis.

With the decline of hunting parties and the advent of breed clubs, selective breeding moved away from practicality and over to extremes. The longest back, largest head or shortest legs became breeders' objectives. Dwarf breeds have been bred for the past one hundred years for these extremes, not for utility. During this period painful arthritis became a serious problem and it will continue to be a potential problem for all dwarfed breeds. It can be diminished through selective breeding to lengthen legs and shorten backs.

78. *And the giants? No dog would grow as big as my biggest relatives. Why did people do this when they know it shortens a big dog's life?*

Well, face facts. Big is impressive. Big gets respect. Big means macho, manly, virile, tough. Big gets results.

Although natural selection favoured dogs smaller than wolves and human intervention in breeding further diminished the wolf-dog's size (so that it was less dangerous in the human settlement), it still retained the genetic potential to return to the size of its founding parents and, under ideal circumstances, to grow even larger than the wolf.

Once the wolf's more sensitive nature, its fearfulness, wariness, prudence and circumspect suspicion had all been diminished, once the wolf had become the dog, breeders were free to add size to their creation. This produced an intimidating weapon. It might have a shortened shelf life but it was certainly effective in its prime. Some of these giant dogs had a natural inclination to be proprietorial, to defend their turf. If they were raised with livestock they protected them from wolves as if the flock were members of the dog's own pack. Big worked.

The colours of certain giant breeds were also carefully chosen by people. It was not a matter of chance. From the Caucasus Mountains of Asia, through Anatolia and then through the mountainous regions of all of Europe, even into west Africa, there are breeds of giant white dogs. These were bred to be the colour of the sheep they guarded. People selected the colour not for aesthetic reasons but for more practical considerations – a white dog blends into a flock of white sheep. It is only when a wolf gets too close that this giant 'sheep' shows its magnificent size and says, 'I ain't no sheep'. The dense coat of these giants, the Caucasian Ovtcharka, Turkish Akbash, Hungarian Kommondor, Polish Tatra Mountain Sheepdog, Slovakian Kuvasz, Italian Maremma, Spanish Pyrenean Mastiff, even the Aidi of the Moroccan Atlas Mountains, was also selected for practical purposes. In fights with wolves the coat protected the skin from wounds. The distribution of these massive white dogs leaves a living trail of migration, trade or invasion routes from Asia into and through Europe thousands of years ago.

79. *If people are so caring and love dogs as much as they say they do, why do they breed me for my looks rather than my own comfort?*

People have the same senses as dogs but the significance of their senses is different. Vision is simply functional for dogs but for people it is their primary aesthetic sense. People are initially attracted to other people by they way they look. Good looks open doors. It is only later, when people use their other senses and listen to, smell and touch the person they are attracted to, that their initial attraction is enhanced or diminished.

People's attraction to dogs is similar. A dog might have the most compatible personality in all of dogdom but unless that dog's physical appearance appeals to someone, the dog does not get considered. Because looks are so important, people now breed dogs primarily for their looks, *then* try to alter their temperament. This is actually a complete inversion of original breeding, when dogs were chosen for their temperament and breeding them happened to produce dogs that looked similar. The unfortunate consequence is that in breeding for looks, people perpetuate shapes and conditions that cause discomfort. Most Yorkshire Terriers have twisted hind legs. Most Cavalier King Charles Spaniels will develop valvular heart disease. Many Pekingese have tight nostrils and slack, soft palates, both of which interfere with breathing. Many West Highland White Terriers have skin allergies. Many Bernese Mountain Dogs get painful chips of cartilage in their joints. The list is endless. Dogs do not complain, something that people can be very good at doing. Because they do not, loving, caring and considerate people do not realize that they are continuing to breed dogs with physical defects. They need to stop and think deeply about what they are doing.

80. *Is that why some dogs are born with no hair?*

Of course. Like other genetic defects, hairlessness will occasionally occur in any species, but the hairless individual, lacking thermal protection, usually dies before reaching the age of reproduction. Not only that, hairless dogs carry a potentially lethal gene. If a hairless dog breeds with a hairless dog it is unlikely to produce pups that go on to breed successfully. The defect naturally dies out.

People kept hairless dogs alive because they were odd, unusual, freaky. Then they learned that hairless dogs make exceptionally useful hot-water bottles. The Chinese, as always, were in the vanguard of this selective breeding, but other hairless breeds were either selectively developed in Africa or reached there from Asia. When Europeans discovered the Americas they came across hairless dogs high in the Peruvian mountains, bred by the Incas to provide night-time warmth.

These dogs were either bred from Asian dogs brought to North America with the original migration of people from Asia into North America, or were brought to Peru by unknown Polynesian or African people who arrived there before Europeans. (The Mexican hairless dog may be indigenous too, or it may be a descendant of hairless African dogs brought to Mexico by the Spaniards.)

Regardless of its origin, hairlessness can only be perpetuated by careful breeding of hairless dogs with others that have coats. Some of the descendants are coated and some are not. Both must be used in future breeding to keep hairlessness 'alive'. In cold climates, in particular, hairlessness is a great disadvantage for dogs. I know. I had a Yorkshire Terrier that once gave birth to a pup with full blond hair only on its face and legs, it was otherwise naked. In the heat of the Canadian summer this little genetic accident lay in direct sunlight and got sunburned. When the weather cooled in the autumn it retreated into a heated cupboard where it spent the winter hating its obligatory outdoor visits and treks through the snow. This little dog was kept alive initially out of human curiosity, then for what people define as compassionate reasons. In other circumstances it might have been selectively bred to perpetuate hairlessness, for monetary reward or personal acclaim. This has been the fate of a similar feline genetic accident, also in Canada, where hairlessness has been odiously perpetuated to produce a severely compromised cat called the Sphinx.

81. *Is it true that Arabs instinctively hate me?*

No. Arabs do not instinctively hate dogs. There is a cultural *antipathy* towards dogs, as I have mentioned, because of the ancient conflict between Islam and Zoroastrianism, but there is another reason for a deep-seated cultural dislike of dogs, one with a profoundly sensible origin – rabies.

Throughout the world today there are 30,000 human rabies casualties each year. Ninety-nine per cent of these cases are contracted through dog bites. This has always been so. When ecological and cultural circumstances permit, as they do today in India and as they once did in Arab countries, the rabies virus thrives in dogs and kills people.

Islam, like its parent religion Judaism, incorporates laws of hygiene into religious observance. Jewish Kosher and Islamic Halal laws, for example, describe what may and may not be eaten. Included in what may not be eaten is a description of tuberculosis lesions in cattle that is as accurate as in any modern veterinary textbook. Other wise individuals, followers of the newer religion, saw there was a relationship between dog bites and people soon dying the hideously painful death of hydrophobia. Once that association was made, contact with dogs was proscribed by religious edict. Islam's antipathy to dogs is based on the prevalence of rabies in the Arabian peninsula fifteen hundred years ago. Contamination with dog saliva, declares Islam, must be followed by a ritual cleansing.

Today, rabies remains a scourge in many Third World countries. If religious leaders were still as sensible as early Moslem leaders and integrated into their religions the need for, say, a ritual anti-rabies vaccination, these needless deaths would be avoided. Even better would be the vaccination of all stray or owned dogs. The World Health Organization has

shown through pilot projects that this is practical and effective, and that the worldwide elimination of dog rabies is possible. Unfortunately, in many countries the greatest obstacles
are people's hidden cultural barriers.

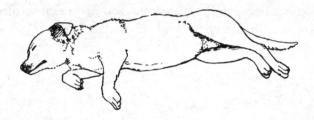

82. *So why have the Bedouin kept Salukis for thousands of years?*

Ah, well. The Bedouins' relationship with their dogs was deeply rooted long before Islam spread throughout the Middle East, the lands of the Bedouin. When the Bedouin converted to Islam they accepted the religious edict that dogs are unclean but, with benignly simple logic, classified their Salukis as 'Salukis', not dogs. These great racing hounds, animals that have accompanied the hawk on hunts for thousands of years, remain partners on the hunt because the relationship between the Saluki and the Bedouin was already too profound and deep to sunder.

83. *I am told that in Japan dogs lead either glorious or pitiful lives. Why is there such a difference in the way they are treated?*

Once more, economic and cultural factors combine to influence both aspects of the dog's life in Japan. Let's set one misconception straight: there has never been an historical tradition of eating dogs in Japan. That is a culinary habit of the neighbouring Koreans and Chinese. The Japanese Buddhist/Shintoist tradition did not permit eating any land mammals and that included dogs.

Japan was a closed culture longer than perhaps any other great nation and it was not until the mid-nineteenth century that it opened its doors to the cultural influence of the rest of the world. During its time of isolation, because domesticated animals were not raised as 'crops' as they were elsewhere in Asia, Europe and Africa, herding and livestock guarding dogs did not evolve as they did elsewhere. And because there was no historical tradition of hunting wild animals, Japanese dogs were not highly bred to sight- or scent-hunt or latterly, as happened in Europe, to set, point and retrieve. (In rural parts of Japan, dogs were actually used to hunt boar and deer but this was done quietly, on the side as it were.) Finally, unlike the far north and parts of Europe such as Belgium and Switzerland, dogs were never used as draught animals in Japan.

This left only a few minor roles for dogs, the most important of which was guarding. A dog's responsibility was to warn of the approach of strangers. Its other role was for amusement, either as a lap dog of the nobility or as a fighting dog of the samurai class. All in all, dogs were quite peripheral to life, much more so than in Western countries. In rural parts of Japan today, and that means in most parts of Japan, the dog remains peripheral to life. If a dog is owned, and many are, it is probably chained to a post in a small yard.

City dogs, on the other hand, often lead deliciously pampered lives. They are fed the best food, given expensive toys, walked daily in the parks. These are Walt Disney creatures come to life. Pets are products of Hollywood. They are icons of Western life and are status symbols. At least, that is what they started out as. The second generation of urban Japanese dog owners melted for the dog's charms and the dog's role for these individuals is the same as elsewhere in Europe, Australasia and North America.

Local culture still impinges even on these cosseted canines. Each culture has its own anathemas and in Japan noise is one of the greatest. Walls are paper thin. Noise travels far. An unfortunate consequence is that dogs in Japan are more likely to have their vocal cords surgically removed than dogs living anywhere else. (Cats, however, almost never have their claws amputated as is so often done in the United States. In Japan that is a cultural taboo.) Only now are some Japanese dog owners learning that careful selection of breeding stock and early training prevent excess barking behaviour from developing.

84. *If you ask me, pigs are as clever as dogs. Why do people eat other animals, such as pigs, but not me?*

Pigs are sociable, just like dogs. Pigs respond to words just like dogs. Pigs learn to use latrine sites for their body waste, just like dogs. Pigs enjoy attention, a tickle behind the ears, just like dogs. But pigs often get eaten. In Britain there are just under seven million dogs; most will live over twelve years. In Britain at any time there are about eight million pigs; virtually all of them will be dead within six months, killed by their keepers or their keepers' contractors and used for food and clothing. People use every part of the pig 'other than its oink', farmers say. They do not say the same about their dogs.

The cleverness or intelligence of a species plays a relatively insignificant role in whether or not an animal is eaten. (To complicate matters, people do not necessarily all mean the same thing when they use a word like 'clever' or 'intelligent'.) The Japanese don't eat rabbit, but the British do. Both nationalities probably accept a rabbit is mentally on a par with a dead newt – certainly not as 'clever' or 'intelligent' as pigs or dogs. The British don't eat horse but the Germans, French and Belgians do. Yet these cultures probably acknowledge that the horse is as 'clever' as or more 'clever' than the pig or dog.

Tradition, and that naturally means religion and superstition, is the motivation for eating some animals but not others. People just do not think about what they are doing. Their eating habits are on autopilot. Increasingly, a large part of the population in Europe and North America, overwhelmingly women in particular, are beginning to question why they eat the way they do. This has led to a significant reduction in people's habit of eating baby animals. For example, veal consumption has plummeted in northern Europe. Dogs are a hidden reason for these changes, for it is through living intimately with dogs that many people first realize that animals other than people also have feelings and emotions. Once people realize that dogs are sentient individuals, they begin to think about pigs. As more people think about what they are doing, more people will change their eating habits.

85. *Do people in all countries and cultures treat dogs the same way? Do politics play a role in my life? Am I a political animal?*

No and yes. Dogs are not treated the same way everywhere. Religious tradition and ethics, economics and politics decide how dogs are treated. You need only look at differences between cultures within a country to see dramatic changes: English-speaking Canadians keep more pets than French-speaking Canadians; French-speaking Belgians keep more pets than Flemish-speaking Belgians; German-speaking Swiss keep more pets than Italian-speaking Swiss.

Numbers can be quite irrelevant to how dogs are actually treated. The per-household ownership of dogs in Eastern European countries is much higher than the average for European Union countries, but that does not mean that Eastern Europe's dogs are treated better or worse.

One explanation for this unexpected European statistic is that under communist rule, Eastern Europe remained more agricultural than the West. Agricultural tradition includes farm dogs. In countries like Poland it is only a generation since people left the farm to work in cities and towns. When they moved they took their traditions with them and this included their dogs.

Under communism, recreational activities were limited. Travel was restricted to a person's own country or other nearby communist countries. Breeding, showing or even walking dogs offered a harmless and enjoyable recreational activity. Under communist regimes, virtually everything needed government sanction. For example, in the former Soviet Union, three people holding a meeting was acceptable, but four people holding a meeting needed a government licence. Dog owning, on the other hand, was looked upon by the government with a curiously lenient eye. Communist governments simply looked the other way and allowed private and illegal dog markets to flourish, permitted people to flout the law openly by importing dogs from the West, breeding them, then meeting publicly or in private to trade, sell or just talk about them. Owning a dog remained one of the few freedoms permitted under communism. At the time of the collapse of the Soviet Union there were more dogs in Moscow than in all of Sweden. There still are.

86. *People talk about the ethical dangers of genetic manipulation but they've been manipulating my kind for centuries. What's the difference?*

People are learning to abhor 'science'. To some, the word 'science' conjures up the same emotional response as the words 'military-industrial complex'. Both denote unmitigated evil.

By creating the dog from the wolf and then by altering the wolf-dog into one-kilogram Chihuahuas and one-hundred-kilogram Mastiffs, people carried out the most spectacular genetic manipulation yet achieved.

This dramatic genetic manipulation was carried out by trial and error. In the process there were countless combinations that did not function as breeders planned and these were discarded. People think of this process as 'unscientific' or 'amateur'. On the contrary, especially during the past hundred years, dog breeding was as 'scientific' and 'professional' as knowledge permitted.

The elucidation of the role of DNA is as important to the future of life on earth as any other 'discovery', for it explains the genetic basis of life. Understanding how genes control not just size and colour but also susceptibility to disease, even temperament, means that what once was carried out by trial and error can now be conducted with more accuracy. For example, science has discovered that a specific gene is responsible for a certain form of blindness in Irish Setters, a blindness caused by progressive retinal atrophy or, 'PRA'.

In its simplest form, genetic manipulation means genetic testing and avoiding breeding from Irish Setters that carry this dangerous gene. Most people accept that concept. In its more controversial form, genetic manipulation means snipping out this dangerous gene from an Irish Setter's germ cells – its eggs or sperm – and splicing in the 'safe' gene related to good eyes or no PRA. Many people feel this is not an ethically acceptable scientific activity. Pragmatically, it is only a faster method of doing what dog breeders have been doing by trial and error for centuries.

There is a completely different concept of genetic manipulation that involves crossing one species that is genetically incompatible with another. Lions and tigers are genetically compatible and if they breed naturally they produce 'tigons'. Genetic engineering is not involved. Goats and sheep do not breed naturally but through genetic engineering it is possible to cross these species and produce 'geep'. This form of genetic manipulation is ethically profoundly different from the accelerated improvement of a species that can be achieved by replacing 'bad' genes with 'good' ones from the same species.

87. *But when people control breeding and create distinct genetic types, don't they know they are reducing my gene pool?*

That is a basic problem not yet appreciated by dog breeders.

There is a magnificent advantage in retaining a large pool of mutts – mongrels, Heinzes, bitsers, random-breds – call them what you like. This is the most delicious genetic soup, a melange that can be dipped into at any time to add a little spice to the restricted genetic pool of a specific breed. Throughout the history of the dog this pool has remained constant. The twentieth century has seen the advent of intensified selective breeding and the creation of about four hundred world-recognized 'breed standards'. Some of these breeds descend from restricted genetic pools. For example, all Bearded Collies descend from a specific mating of two dogs in the mid-1940s. Virtually all Nova Scotia Duck Tolling Retrievers, more popular in Sweden than in their native Canada, descend from similar narrow blood lines. If there are 'bad' genes in the parent stock, all the descendants carry these genes, embedding the defect permanently in the breed. By reducing the dog's genetic pool to four hundred distinct groups, the genetic soup from which improvements come would become thin and watery.

88. *So what's the future for me? Will people have more dogs?*

Not likely, although there will be local increases in the dog population. As the population of North America and Europe ages, the number of dogs will decrease. These regions became saturated by dogs in the 1980s and are already experiencing a drop in dog population.

The population of Japan is ageing just as quickly as Europe's but in Japan the dog population will increase for another generation before it reaches a plateau. This will happen because dog ownership is still in its expansion stage among the younger population.

China is the world's big question mark. This is where it all began, probably where wolf-dogs were first selectively bred, where both miniaturization and dwarfing first occurred. This is the native home of the lap dog, the mother land for soft, warm furries everywhere. While eighteenth-century Imperial Palace pups were suckled by imperial wet nurses and tended by palace eunuchs, in the rest of China dogs were classified as hunting dogs, watch dogs or edible dogs. Among China's rulers, as elsewhere among rulers, companion dogs were the prerogative of the elite.

Under Mao's leadership, dog owning was proscribed. Today it is still severely restricted. In Beijing numbers are restricted through the highest dog-licence fee in the world, yet still Beijing's inhabitants keep dogs – hundreds of thousands of them. As China moves to become the world's leading industrial giant, the demand for dog ownership among the new emerging entrepreneurial elite will be no different in quality from the demand felt in Europe and Japan. But what a difference in quantity; there are perhaps two hundred million dogs throughout the world, thirty-five million in the United States, but only an estimated fifteen million in China. With a population five times that of the United States, the dog's potential future in China is quite simply its biggest future.

89. *What will we be like? What hidden plans do people have for us?*

This depends upon where dogs live, but let's assume they live anywhere in Europe, Australasia or North America, or in any of the affluent cities of the world.

Non-city dogs have a pretty good future. They will continue to provide people with a living link to the land and an emotional link with the past. Their freedom of movement will be restricted but they will continue to be selectively bred to work on farms and ranches as herders, shepherds, guards and heelers. They will continue to be selectively bred to follow scent trails, although they may find that in the future they will be following aniseed trails instead of following the trails of real game. Country dogs will find there are fewer packs to join to hunt for sport.

Throughout continental Europe, especially Eastern Europe, and in North America, country dogs will continue to enjoy doing 'guy' things with men. They will be selectively bred to look good as well as to hunt efficiently and, more than ever before, they will accompany their masters home to be fed nutritious food and sleep in warm beds.

City dogs face a less certain future. People will become increasingly prissy about their hygiene and more critical of dog droppings. Dog populations will fall but, more importantly, dog characteristics will change. Keeping dogs will continue to be a habit of the more nurturing and caring portion of the population. These extra-sensitive people are more prone to 'care-eliciting' dog behaviour. One consequence will be an increase in dogs that scream 'I'm helpless!', either morphologically through exaggerated infant features like large eyes and big heads, or behaviourally, by acting dependent and helpless.

90. *Final question and it's a bit philosophical: can people survive without me and my companions?*

I am afraid the answer is yes. Dogs are quite expendable.

Some people think that keeping dogs is popular because people have a residual notion that it is still a good thing to do. At one time it certainly was. Dogs were central to people's successful exploration and exploitation of many parts of the world: people would never have survived their migration to the far north without dogs; it is likely that they would not have inhabited the mountainous regions of Asia and Europe without them; it may even be possible that the Polynesians would not have settled the Pacific islands from Hawaii to Easter Island to New Zealand if they had not had dogs and pigs to accompany them to provide a guaranteed source of food during their travels.

Today, dogs may be good for people's health but that does not mean they are irreplaceable. Social support from other people is better for people's good health. It is only because people have lost or forgotten the granite-hard benefits of family and friends that dogs filled the void.

People can survive quite nicely without dogs but in doing so they cut themselves off from one of their last animate links with the natural world. In that sense their quality of life suffers in the absence of canine companions, and quality of life is becoming increasingly important for people.

People are in the midst of one of their greatest ever cultural shifts. For their entire existence on earth they have simply used the earth's resources. Many Western people are of the opinion that they are abusers of nature while more enlightened 'primitive' people such as native Americans lived in harmony with nature. This is puerile drivel. So-called primitive people were just as destructive, they simply did not have the tools of destruction that industrial groups have.

More recently, large numbers of affluent people with full bellies have questioned what their ancestors did, and they continue to do so. The dog looks on bemused while people invest millions of dollars to free whales trapped by winter ice or push sick dolphins back into the ocean. People are willing to do these things because of the dramatic cultural shift away from looking upon animals as a source of exploitation, nourishment, clothing or labour. The dog sits quietly while people think about their radically new relationship with nature, one in which nature is treasured for social and psychological rather than practical and utilitarian reasons.

The dog benefits from people's perceptual changes. In law a dog remains the property of its owner but in the future dogs will be classified as more than simply 'chattels'. This legal change first occurred in 1979 in the Civil Court of the State of New York when a judge, Seymour Friedman, passed judgment saying, 'This court now overrules precedent and holds that a pet is not just a thing, but occupies a special place somewhere between a person and a piece of personal property'. The following year a judge in California instituted a similar new interpretation when he overruled a will asking for a pet dog to be destroyed by saying that a dog is 'a very special type of personal property' and that the legal purpose of a will cannot include the destruction of this form of personal property.

Dogs may not know it but in this hidden change in people's perception of the world, the dog wins, for it is part of the natural world that people want to preserve. This improves the quality of life of people and that improves the future for dogs.

INDEX